BERLITZ®

KT-403-834

NEW ZEALAND

10th edition (1995/1996)

Berlitz Trademark Reg. U.S. Patent Office and other countries.
Marca Registrada. Library of Congress Catalog Card No. 84-080845.

Printed in Switzerland by Weber S.A., Bienne.

How to use our guide

- All the practical information, hints and tips you will need before and during the trip start on p. 107.

- For general background, see the sections The Land and the People, p. 6 and A Brief History, p. 15.

- All the sights to see are listed between pp. 25 and 90. Our own choice of sights most highly recommended is pin-pointed by the Berlitz symbol.

- Sports, entertainment and other leisure activities are described between pp. 91 and 102, while information on restaurants and cuisine is to be found on pp. 102 to 106.

- Finally, there is an index at the back of the book, pp. 126-128.

Although we make every effort to ensure the accuracy of all the information in this book, changes occur incessantly. We cannot therefore take responsibility for facts, prices, addresses and circumstances in general that are constantly subject to alteration. Our guides are updated on a regular basis as we reprint, and we are always grateful to readers who let us know of any errors, changes or serious omissions they come across.

Text: Catherine McLeod
Staff Editor: Christina Jackson
Photography: Walter Imber. Cover photo and pp. 7, 26 Jon Davison; p. 41 Jacky Reymond; pp. 54, 94 Ronald McLeod; pp. 72, 76, 95 Marka srl; p. 80 Georg Stärk.
Layout: Doris Haldemann
We wish to thank the New Zealand Tourist and Publicity Department, Air New Zealand and Mount Cook Airlines for their help with this guide. We're especially grateful to Graeme Hay, Joseph Frahm, Marion Fisher and Ralph Lenton for information and assistance.
Cartography: Falk-Verlag, Hamburg.

Contents

The Land and the People

New Zealand lies in the blue of the Pacific, midway between the Equator and the South Pole. On a map of the world it looks like a small question mark drawn on the vastness of the ocean. Two narrow strips of land, referred to simply as the North Island and the South Island, make up most of the territory. Stewart Island forms the dot at the bottom of the question mark. The continent of Australia sprawls 1,500 kilometres to the north-west; 2,300 kilometres to the south stretch the icy wastes of Antarctica.

Almost all New Zealanders are born within sight of the sea, and certainly within reach of it. From the air you can watch it curling in magnificent strength around broken shorelines, thundering onto great stretches of deserted beach, or idling peacefully into sheltered inlets and calm

bays. The land – largely hilly, often ruggedly mountainous – is almost unbelievably green, except in the South Island, where the grain fields of the Canterbury Plains shine gold at harvest time and the perennial snows glisten white on the Southern Alps. Long ago the Maoris, approaching New Zealand by sea in their canoes, named it well: Aotearoa, 'Land of the Long White Cloud'.

More than a pastoral country of rolling farmland and flocks of sheep, New Zealand packs a whole variety of climates and landscapes into its 269,000 square kilometres. The north is subtropical, with slow, tidal estuaries half-consolidated by mangrove swamps, stands of native trees – including the aristocratic kauri – flourishing orange and kiwifruit orchards and sweeping beaches. The rippling dunes of

The local store has everything you need, including a warm welcome.

Ninety Mile Beach stretch to land's end at Cape Reinga, a place so magnificently desolate that even hardened travellers may be tempted to believe it is the 'leaping-off place of the spirits' spoken of in Maori legend. The Rotorua lakeland hisses with thermal steam and bubbling mud. Hawke's Bay, tranquil as an English garden, is a pleasant parkland of poplars, weeping willows and pasture kept in perfect trim by thousands of sheep.

The South Island boasts some of the most spectacular scenery: the Alps, stretching for 650 unbroken kilometres, topped by the constantly changing beauty of Mt Cook, the 'Cloud-Piercer' of the Maoris; Tasman Glacier, one of the largest glaciers outside the polar regions; and the forests, fiords, lakes and waterfalls of the far south, still partly unexplored.

When the first European settlers arrived in the early 19th century, they found the country populated by Maoris, a Polynesian people of Caucasian origin whose poetic oral history relates tales of heroic canoe migrations south and east across the Pacific. Driven by hard times, ambition, missionary zeal, or the simple desire to raise their families in a promising 'new' land, the settlers set to work burning the bush and cultivating the soil. They felled the centuries-old kauris for use as masts, tore at the hill faces to sow grass and planted gorse hedges which, in the mild climate, took off across the countryside and grew into miniature forests. Fortunately, the dangers were seen just in time. The pioneers, isolated and homesick, had tried to create another England. In the end, their efforts contributed to the country's heritage. The gorse is still a farmer's nightmare, but arum lilies growing wild on riverbanks and in fields shine ghostly-white against the dark background of native trees. Oaks thrive in New Zealand as they do in Devon villages, and a suburban garden is likely to be a delightful idyll of banana plants and roses, cottage hollyhocks and tropical bougainvillea, planted within sight of indigenous trees like the yellow-flowering kowhai, the glossy leaved karaka and giant native ferns.

There are no wild mammals on the islands, except for introduced species such as pig and

Lacy ferns and a veil of water – a typical bushland scene.

deer, but bird and marine life flourishes. The flightless, nocturnal kiwi is the national bird; and Kiwi, in slang, has come to mean a New Zealander. There are also plump wood-pigeons, nectar-sipping tuis, fearless little fantails which often dart into the house, bell-birds, iridescent kingfishers and rare white herons, whose flight, for the Maoris, is charged with mystic significance. Even in town you're likely to fall asleep to the sound of the more-pork owl, so-named for its mournful call. There are no snakes. Insects thrive, but the only dangerous species is the very rare katipo spider, found in driftwood on some beaches. Keep an eye out for the sandflies, though – they'll nip the wits out of you if you don't use insect repellent. (Don't pay any attention to the story of the sandfly that carried a tourist away – the correct version is that it took two sandflies to do it, and they had both won weightlifting medals at the Olympics.)

Farming and forestry provide the bulk of the country's income. Some 9 million head of cattle and 70 million sheep graze their way across New Zealand's pastures. Carefully developed agricultural techniques have made it possible for the country to exploit the benefits of generous sunshine and rainfall on a terrain which is not, on the whole, arable.

Some 3 million people live in New Zealand and, of them, about 300,000 claim Maori descent.

The Maori and Pakeha (European) populations enjoy the same rights of citizenship and live in harmony and equality under the law. An awareness of Maori culture through education is a binding force and gives an added

A ghost of a moon over Mt Cook, sentinel of the Alps.

sense of identity to all New Zealanders who, irrespective of race, grow up with a knowledge of Maori legend. Such was not **11** always the case. *Maoritanga* (Maori culture) was long submerged by the dominant English culture. Apart from the English and a large number of Scots and Irish, many Dalmatian and Dutch immigrants have settled in New Zealand. Pacific Islanders, especially from the Cook Islands, Western Samoa and Tonga, add variety to the scene.

English is the first language, but the Maori tongue, formerly in danger of dying out, can be studied at school. New Zealand has its own brand of English, its own accent and a home-grown vocabulary rich in irreverent humour, with a sprinkling of Maori words. The forest is the 'bush', a 'bach' is a beach house and 'up the boo-hai' means somewhere up the back of beyond. 'Cow cockies' are dairy farmers. Watch out for 'skites' (show-offs), people who 'poke the borax' (send you up) and the fellow who mysteriously announces it's his 'turn to shout'. He's offering to buy the next round of drinks.

Isolated in their sea-girt country but often widely travelled, New Zealanders are recognizably, outspokenly, themselves. They plant their town squares with spiky, native flax and the plain, almost ugly cabbage-tree, whose unprepossessing leaves hide a flower with a scent so exquisite that the mere memory of it haunts New Zealanders far from home. Having finally turned their backs on the steamed puddings and roasts of their cold-country origins, they blend a cornucopia of subtropical fruits (passion fruit, kiwifruit, feijoas, loquats, tamarillos and guavas) into new, adventurous recipes – and were doing so long before French *nouvelle cuisine* set the seal of gastronomic approval on such practices. New Zealand wine is coming along nicely, too, and carrying off international medals these days. The New Zealand flag with its distinctive Southern Cross flutters proudly from houses and commercial buildings.

New Zealanders are well educated and claim a fair number of famous names for so small a population, from Lord Rutherford, who split the atom, to Dame Kiri Te Kanawa, international opera star; from Katherine Mansfield, the short-story writer, to Sir Edmund Hillary, first to conquer Mt Everest. New Zealanders tend to be egalitarian, competitive and frighteningly fit. No wonder they produced the famous All Black rugby team. They're also friendly and down-to-earth. You'll find a New Zealand lawyer happily patching up the roof of his house over the weekend, while his dentist wife paints the living-room or sprays the fruit trees in the garden. Traditional practicality is one of the reasons why crafts like weaving and pottery flourish.

The sporting opportunities are endless, from white-water rafting and skiing to hunting and fishing. There are hundreds of tennis courts, golf courses, cricket pitches and football grounds. Everybody seems to jog; swimming is a way of life and boats are as much taken for granted as cars. Horse-racing is nothing less than a national hobby – as you'll realize if you encounter race-day traffic.

To get the maximum out of your visit, you should walk the scenic tracks, try the farm holidays, fish the trout streams, fly out to the glaciers. The very distances that kept New Zealand off the well-beaten tourist track have protected it. It's a whole natural experience, waiting to be lived.

New Zealand's national bird, the kiwi, is shy, flightless and rarely seen in the wild.

Facts and Figures

Geography: New Zealand lies south-east of Australia, in the Pacific Ocean. There are two principal islands, the North Island and the South Island, as well as Stewart Island, Chatham Islands and various small outlying islands. From north to south, New Zealand extends for 1,750km. Its area, excluding territories overseas, is 269,057 sq km. One-third of the country is grassland, one-third marginal agricultural land, the remainder mountainous. Highest point: Mt Cook (3,764m).

Population: 3.4 million, of which 81.2 per cent are of European (mostly British) origin; 9 per cent are Maori, and 3 per cent other Polynesian.

Capital: Wellington (pop. 330,000).

Major cities: Auckland (860,000), Christchurch (300,000), Dunedin (110,000), Hamilton (170,000), Napier-Hastings (112,000).

Government: Parliamentary monarchy. The Head of State is Queen Elizabeth II, represented by the Governor-General. Parliament consists of the House of Representatives, comprising 97 members who are elected by the people for three years. Major political parties: National and Labour.

Religion: Anglicans, Presbyterians and Roman Catholics form the majority, but there are representatives of almost all the Christian denominations and other religions, too.

Language: English is the official language. Maori is also spoken.

Economy: New Zealand is the world's third largest producer of wool, the largest producer of lamb and mutton, and the largest exporter of dairy products. Beef production is on the increase. Exports of forest products are now the country's second most important export earner. Fruit, including a number of semi-tropical varieties, is exported. Grain, tobacco and hops are grown for home consumption. Light-engineering industries are expanding. Tourism is a major source of income.

A Brief History

The Maoris have their own account of creation. In the beginning, they say, was the void, containing nothing. This nothingness brought forth a darkness in which the first gods – Papa and Rangi, the Earth Mother and Sky Father, clung together in a passionate embrace. Their children, crushed between them, were desperate for light and air. Tu, god of war, wanted to kill his parents, but Tane, god of nature, intervened and pushed his father far up into the heavens, where Rangi still sheds rainstorms of tears for his lost wife. Her sighs are the mists that rise from the land.

Then Tane took red clay and formed a woman. He breathed life into her and she became his wife. Their daughter was Hine Titama, the Dawn Maiden, by whom Tane had other children. When the Dawn Maiden realized that their relationship was incestuous, she fled into the underworld, where she became the Great Lady of Darkness and, ultimately, goddess of death.

In time a strong and clever child was born. His name was Maui. One day he fished the whole of the North Island out of the sea with the aid of a magic jawbone. This mighty catch was known as Te Ika a Maui, 'Maui's Fish', the old name for the North Island. If you look at a map, you see the fish-hook of Maui in the curve of Hawke Bay, and the fish's eye in the circle of Lake Taupo. Maui warned his brothers to leave the fish alone, but he had no sooner turned his back than they began hacking at the huge creature, creating the valleys and mountains that exist today.

Maui failed in his greatest undertaking. He set out to find the Great Lady of Darkness asleep in the underworld. He turned himself into a caterpillar, hoping to enter her womb and emerge from her mouth, thus overcoming death for all time. All living creatures were anxious to help, but a skittish little bird, Piwakawaka the fantail, found the whole thing so funny that his nervous twitters disturbed the goddess. She woke with a start and crushed Maui between her thighs. So ended man's quest for immortality.

Of Moas and Maoris

Around AD 750 New Zealand was inhabited by Archaic Maoris or Moa Hunters, Stone Age fishermen and hunters of Polynesian origin who lived on the east coast of the South Island. (*Moa* is the Polynesian word for 'fowl', but in New Zealand it was applied to the huge prehistoric birds which were hunted for food.)

Maori tradition doesn't make any mention of these early inhabitants. Instead it relates that the first visitor to these parts was a Polynesian named Kupe, who found the islands deserted in the 10th century. Kupe did not settle but returned to a place called Hawaiki, where he gave directions for reaching the new land. This story probably contains a grain of truth. It also raises many questions. Hawaiki, which means 'homeland', cannot be traced to any island or group of islands. For the Maoris of New Zealand, Hawaiki probably refers to Tahiti or the Marquesas Islands.

It is generally accepted that the Maoris came from South China via the East Indies, which would account for the similarities between the Maori and Malay languages. There may also have been a separate drift of people from the Americas – the only

Bold navigators and warriors, the Maori perfected carving and the art of frightening enemies.

explanation to date for the existence of plants such as the sweet potato in New Zealand.

Maori lore tells of the 'Great Migration', in the 14th century, when a fleet of large canoes reached the islands of Aotearoa ('Land of the Long White Cloud') or Tiritiri o te Moana ('Gift of the Sea'). Maoris traditionally trace their ancestry to the occupants of these canoes. These Classic Maoris built fortified villages. They engaged in intertribal warfare and brought carving to a high art. They lived mostly on birds, fish, fern roots and berries and cultivated taro and sweet potato *(kumara)*, supplementing their diet with human flesh. Cannibalism, possibly arising from dietary need, later took on a ritual significance.

In Classic Maori society the tribe *(iwi)*, presided over by a chief *(ariki)*, was divided into a number of smaller units *(hapu)*. Major issues that affected the tribe were debated in the *marae*, or village meeting-place, where public speaking reached heights of rhetoric, as it still does today. High priests received a rigorous training in tribal history and ritual, including the imposition and lifting of *tapu* – a broad term

meaning, among other things, 'holy' or 'forbidden'. Although influenced by superstition, *tapu* fostered everything from hygiene and morality to the preservation of fishing grounds. The concept of *mana* (prestige) was of great   **17** importance and often led to war, with much hand-to-hand fighting and the use of spears, clubs and throwing sticks. Prisoners often ended up as slaves. The least affront to a tribe's *mana* could lead to an *utu*, or vendetta, lasting for generations.

The First Europeans

In 1642 Abel Janszoon Tasman became the first European to sight New Zealand. He had been sent in search of the great unknown southern continent, *Terra Australis Incognita*, by the Dutch East India Company. Although Tasman never set foot on shore, he charted part of the west coast. He called the country Staten Landt, later changed to Nieuw Zeeland after a Dutch province.

Then in 1769 the English explorer James Cook circumnavigated New Zealand, and after him came the Frenchmen Jean-François Marie de Surville and Marion du Fresne. News of the discovery attracted adventurers, traders, sealers and whalers, who kidnapped Maoris, broke their laws and introduced disease and firearms. Enraged, the Maoris killed and ate the crew members of two ships. The ensuing reports of 'heathen' gourmandize and Western degeneracy proved unpalatable to the Reverend Samuel Marsden, missionary and magistrate in the Australian colony of New South Wales.

Under the aegis of the Anglican Church Missionary Society, Marsden established mission stations in New Zealand, and he preached the first Christian sermon there on Christmas Day, 1814. The Maoris were slow to respond. Nine years elapsed before a convert was made. The

Northland chief Hongi Hika protected the missionaries but remarked disparagingly that the religion wasn't likely to catch on: it wouldn't work for warriors.

The availability of guns gave fresh impetus to warring chiefs. The 1820s and 1830s witnessed horrifying intertribal bloodshed. Meanwhile, the church itself was divided, as each denomination strove to promote its own brand of Christianity. For their part, the Maoris revelled in the arguments and commented ironically on the race to win souls. They nevertheless converted in increasing numbers, some seeing the message of the church as a reprieve from the ceaseless destruction of *utu*, others feeling, perhaps, that the old gods had been superseded.

By 1831 fear of French annexation had been added to existing problems of general lawlessness,

The next generation pays tribute to New Zealand's pioneers.

along with atrocities against the Maoris and Maori reprisals. As a result, the missionaries were able to persuade a number of influential chiefs to send a plea for protection to the British crown.

Britain's response was the appointment of a Resident in the person of James Busby. His declared aim was the conciliation of all groups, but he proved ill-fitted to the task and in 1838 the office was discontinued. Instead Captain William Hobson was appointed lieutenant-governor, and British land in New Zealand was administered as a dependency of the colony of New South Wales.

It was Hobson who drafted the Treaty of Waitangi, signed February 6, 1840, by which the Maoris ceded sovereignty to the British crown in exchange for law and order and the rights of ownership to tribal lands. Some 50 Maori chiefs put their hand to the treaty; by June over 450 additional signatures had been collected from outlying districts. But it is doubtful whether the majority understood the meaning of their action. To the Maoris, giving away the land was inconceivable since, although areas changed occupants, the land belonged to everyone – it was Papa, the Earth Mother.

The Crown had the sole right to purchase land; and large-scale European settlement now began, greatly encouraged by the establishment in Britain of the New Zealand Company, which hoped to create a model colony.

Conflict and Development

While the Maoris had not grasped the significance of the Treaty of Waitangi, the Europeans had underestimated Maori attachment to the land. So began a period of intermittent land disputes between Maoris and Europeans, which led to the Land Wars of the 1860s and wracked the country for 40 years. Accounts of Pakeha speculation, ignorant administration and bewilderment, and of Maori heroism, desperation and occasional collaboration make bitter reading.

The King Movement, started by a chief called Wiremu Tamihana, attempted to achieve unity among the Maoris by establishing a monarchy. Had the Maoris united successfully, they might have won the day, but up against lethal British artillery and practising an outdated code of individualistic chivalry, it was not to be. Hardest of all, when the fighting was over, the 'rebels' were punished for their efforts by the confiscation of yet more land. By 1892 the Maori people were left with only 4½ million hectares, much of it useless for farming.

While the North Island lived through these unhappy years, the South Island, with its small Maori population, was relatively free from conflict and ripe for development. The discovery of gold in 1861 by an Australian, Gabriel Read, put the South Island on the map. The metal was found in the rivers of Otago province. Almost overnight thousands of immigrants poured into New Zealand. Gold became the country's major export, and Dunedin – a flourishing, Scots-dominated commercial and banking centre – its largest town. The boom was over by 1870, but for a brief period the Shotover was known as the 'richest river in the world'. Within a decade foodstuffs had replaced gold as the main export. The installation of refrigeration in cargo ships made it possible to transport meat and dairy products over long distances to foreign markets. The compass for New Zealand's future was set.

Meanwhile, under the Constitution of 1852, drafted by Governor George Grey, the people of New Zealand achieved a measure of self-government with the introduction of an elected House of Representatives. Six Provincial Councils and the superintendents of the provinces were also elected directly. The British monarch remained the Head of State; and the governor, appointed by London, was to nominate the members of the Legislative Council, who held office for life.

Elections were held in 1855 and 1856, and a number of picturesque and able men succeeded one another as prime minister. However, only individual landowners could vote, so the Maoris were effectively excluded. The franchise, slightly liberalized in 1867, was later extended to all men aged 21 and over. Then, in 1893, New Zealand women became among the first in the world to gain the vote.

King Dick and Company

For more than ten years, until his death in 1906, a benevolent liberal, Richard John Seddon, served as the country's prime minister. Familiarly known as King Dick, he made New Zealand famous as a humanitarian democracy. Political theorists from Europe flocked to marvel at the application of ideas which, in older societies, **21** remained on paper. In addition to women's suffrage, old-age benefits and compulsory state arbitration in industrial disputes were introduced. It was Seddon who coined the phrase 'God's Own Country' (since irreverently reduced to 'Godzone') to describe New Zealand.

In 1914 New Zealand entered the war on the side of Britain. The heroism of New Zealand and Australian troops during the campaign in the Dardanelles left indelible memories. April 25, the date of the landing at Gallipoli, was declared a national holiday. Now dedicated to all of the country's armed forces, it owes its name, ANZAC Day, to the Australian and New Zealand Army Corps. New Zealand's casualties during World War I totalled 58,000 – one in seventeen of the population. After the war, an influenza epidemic took a further 5,500 lives. From the tragedy of these losses there emerged a new sense of nationhood. The country entered the League of Nations as an independent member.

From Hunger to Humanity

The Great Depression dealt a savage blow to New Zealand, a small country dependent on overseas markets. Exports fell 40 per cent in just two years. The government 'balanced' the budget by cutting down drastically on public expenditure. Since the then prime minister was opposed to 'pay without work', unemployed men cleared scrub from the roadsides, planted trees and drained swamps. There was rioting, looting, stealing and even cases of real hunger.

When the Labour Party came to power, in 1935, they instituted a social security system and comprehensive medical services, as well as state-financed housing schemes. Once again New Zealand took the lead as a country which believed in equality. Not only were the Maoris eligible for all these benefits, in an attempt to equalize standards of living they were given more help than citizens of European descent.

During World War II more than 140,000 New Zealanders served overseas, in Europe and the Middle East. Some 11,000 lost their lives. In 1947 the country gained the right to amend the Constitution without reference to Britain, and the Legislative Council was abolished in 1950. Today Parliament consists of a single chamber, the House of Represen-

tatives, with 92 elected members; New Zealand is a member of the British Commonwealth; and a governor-general, usually a New Zealander, represents the Queen.

If the country can be said to have a problem, it is the rate of emigration. 'Overseas' is still a magic word, holding promise of better jobs and salaries, of recognition for performers and artists, and a rather more cosmopolitan

Get together – races mix in an atmosphere of mutual respect.

lifestyle than is sustainable in a country of 3½ million inhabitants. Yet New Zealanders seldom lose their sense of identity. Gradually, with effort and goodwill, a nation has been forged that sees home not as the soft turf of England but as the verdant hills and seaswept beaches of New Zealand. **23**

Where to Go

To get the most out of a New Zealand holiday you'll want to visit both islands. A month gives time for a leisurely view.

An ideal basic itinerary would start at Auckland, with road excursions to Northland and Central North Island. Ferries link the two islands between the capital, Wellington, and Picton, centre of the Marlborough Sounds area. Or you can fly direct to Christchurch for a combined fly-drive tour of the scenic highlights of the South Island – Mt Cook in the Southern Alps and then on to Queenstown and Fiordland.

The North Island

There's an amazing variety of scenery and interest packed into the country's northern land-mass. Preserved in the area around the Bay of Islands are memories of New Zealand's turbulent past. Steaming thermal activity, lakeside attractions and an insight into Maori culture draw visitors to Central North Island. To the south stands fiery Mt Ngauruhoe and the skier's playground of Ruapehu. There are big cities, too: rapidly expanding Auckland and cosmopolitan Wellington.

Auckland

More than 850,000 people reside in Auckland, the Queen City of New Zealand and the country's largest metropolis by far, beautifully positioned on a narrow isthmus. To the west lie the shallow waters of Manukau Harbour, navigable only to small ships. Waitemata Harbour to the east is a 'Sea of Sparkling Water' indented with bays and inlets and scattered over with islands. One of them, Rangitoto, a volcano active until only 200 years ago, stands guard at the harbour entrance.

Auckland is a highly appealing blend of the colonial and the modern, the provincial and the cosmopolitan. From the commercial centre near the waterfront, the city rises in ridges, punctuated by a series of small volcanic cones which lend character to the landscape and provide natural breathing-space. The terraces that ring many of the cones were built by the Maoris, who surrounded their fortified villages with ditches and earth ramparts.

Auckland's climate is mild but changeable. Sunlight can switch without warning to a down pour. So, however reassuring the sky seems in the morning, it's always wisest to carry a raincoat.

A land of contrasts – ranging from timeless lunar landscapes to innovative urban design.

Waitemata Harbour is New Zealand's largest port. Each year, at the end of January, the world's largest one-day yachting event, the Anniversary Day Regatta, is held here. The race celebrates the foundation of the city in 1840 as capital of the country – a title it lost 25 years later to Wellington. Curving over the harbour, **Auckland Harbour Bridge** links the city to the North Shore suburbs. From it you'll catch a glimpse of Westhaven Boat Harbour, one of the world's biggest yacht basins. You can drive over the bridge or take the ferry to picturesque Devonport. Starting from here, a succession of good beaches loops northward up the east coast.

City Sightseeing

Start your sightseeing at the Ferry Buildings, terminus for boats to various points in the Hauraki Gulf. From here, **Queen Street** cuts right through the centre of town. In the area is the restored **Customs House**, built in French Renaissance style by Thomas Mahoney in 1888. Have a look at the Victorian interior, now filled with up-to-the-minute boutiques.

The **Town Hall**, a stone building, at the corner of Grey's Avenue and Queen Street, fronts on Aotea Square. Step inside to view the largest chunk of kauri timber in existence.

The **Central Public Library** (Lorne Street) contains some rare documents and manuscripts, on view by prior arrangement only. Its treasures include papers relating to Captain Cook's voyage of exploration, Governor George Grey's library (over 15,000 volumes), some 11th-century Greek manuscripts, Shakespeare's first folio (1623), and the largest collection of Alexandre Dumas manuscripts outside the Bibliothèque Nationale in Paris.

Auckland City Art Gallery, in Wellesley Street East, exhibits works with a New Zealand connection. The collection includes a painting by William Hodges, who accompanied Captain Cook to New Zealand, and a variety of 19th- and 20th-century paintings and sculptures, including works by the celebrated New Zealand painter Frances Hodgkins.

Albert Park is a favourite lunch-hour spot for office workers and students. It is overlooked by the crenellated Neo-Gothic tower of Auckland University. If you've a taste for Victorian architectural fantasies, take a look at the **Supreme Court** (1868) in Waterloo Quadrant, built to resemble Warwick Castle in England, complete with dour turrets and unlikely gargoyles.

Wander the **Domain**, a green precinct of playing fields and gardens in the heart of Auckland. A spring feeds the pond where New Zealand's first rainbow trout were hatched from Californian stock. Take time to visit the enchanting Winter Garden, with its Tropical and Cool houses; and the Garden for the Blind, where plants are chosen for their scent rather than their colour.

The **Auckland War Memorial Museum**, an ethnological and natural history collection, stands on a rise in the Domain. You'll need at least an hour to see the highlights: an authentic Maori meeting-house (1878), a carved gateway and a magnificent old war canoe, 25 metres long. Proud portraits of Maori chiefs by C.F. Goldie (1870-1947) add a human dimension to the ethnological displays; native species fill the Hall of New Zealand Birds.

Leaving the Domain by the Parnell Road exit, you enter the restored colonial elegance of **Parnell**, a smart Auckland suburb. Not so long ago the quarter had slipped down in the world; now the boutiques, cafés and restaurants of Parnell village sparkle with new life. The residents take pride in a colonial-style bank and the old Cathedral Church of St Mary (1888), a delightful wooden construction.

South of the Domain, **Mt Eden**, Auckland's highest point,

AUCKLAND

Waitemata Harbour

Freemans Bay

N

| 0 | 200 | 400 m |
| 0 | 200 | 400 yards |

Launch Steps

Western Viaduct

Quay St.

EEMANS BAY

Central Post Office

Bus Terminal

Customs St.

Quay Street

Sturdee St.

Customs Street West

Hobson St.

Lower Albert St.

Quay Street

Powerhouse Lane

Tinley St.

nshawe Street

Nelson Street

Hobson Street

Swanson St.

Queen Street

Fort Street

Bank of New Zealand

Shortland St.

Emily

Beach

Anzac

Avenue

Auckland Railway Station

MELANESIAN MISSION MUSEUM

St. Patrick's Cathedral

Kingston St.

Durham St. W.

High Street

Chancery St.

Eden Crescent

C I T Y

Victoria Street West

Federal St.

Albert St.

Elliot St.

Queen Street

Victoria St. Easter

Bowen Avenue

Princes

Waterloo Quadrant

Supreme Court

St.

PARNELL

Wellesley Street West

Lorne St.

Kitchener

Old Government House

Albert Park

Symonds

Wynyard

St.

St. Andrew's Church

Alten Road

Churchill

Gittos St.

HOLY TRINITY CATHEDRAL

Central public Library

Auckland Information Centre

Drive

Wellesley St. East

Lorne St.

Rutland St.

Art Gallery

Princes

Alfred St.

Symonds

Road

Stanley

Carlaw Park

lice Station

Mayoral Avenue

Vincent St.

Town Hall

Wakefield St.

Airdale Street

Paul Street

Symonds Street

Grafton Road

Auckland

AND TECHNOLOGY

Myers Park

Greys

Street

Waverley St.

Turner St.

Lyndock Mt. St.

St.

Cully

Domain

Liverpool Road

City Road

Grafton

Grafton Road

Drive

Queen

Symonds

Karangahape Rd.

ross St.

NEWTOWN

Upper Queen

Grafton Bridge

Grafton Road

Domain

War Memorial Museum

ONE TREE HILL DOMAIN

MT. EDEN

Winter Gardens

rises 196 metres above the city. The Maoris call the volcanic cone Maungawhau, 'Tree-Clad Mountain'. A fortified village stood here as far back as the 12th century. From the summit there's a perfect view into the crater and out in all directions over the city.

Another volcanic cone, **One Tree Hill** in Cornwall Park, provides more magnificent views. Sir John Logan Campbell, the 'Father of Auckland', is buried on the summit, not far from an obelisk which he raised in admiration of the Maori race.

Visitors flock to the **Zoological Gardens**, in Motions Road, for a close look at New Zealand's flightless national bird, the kiwi. (There are three kiwi species, all of which display the same basic characteristics.) You'll also want to see the slow, awkward tuatara, a lizard-like reptile that has survived without modification since the time of the dinosaurs. Both tuatara and kiwi receive their visitors in the Nocturnal House.

The **Museum of Transport and Technology** (Motat), alongside the zoo, delights machinery buffs. There's a working tramway and a colonial village, plus displays on computers, photography, printing and aircraft.

A pleasant drive along the **waterfront** takes in Okahu Bay, Savage Memorial Park with its monument to Michael Savage, the country's first Labour prime minister, and Mission Bay, where the former Melanesian Mission House now serves as a museum devoted to Melanesian artefacts.

For an eyeball-to-eyeball encounter with the local marine life, visit **Kelly Tarlton's Underwater World** at Orakei Wharf, on Tamaki Drive. Moving walkways transport visitors through acrylic tunnels for a marvellous undersea view of sharks, rays, colourful fish and other marine creatures.

Auckland Environs
Hauraki Gulf, site of the country's first maritime park, is a vast area of sheltered water between the mainland and Coromandel Peninsula. Dozens of islands lie

Piha's black sands offer surfing and splendid isolation.

within the park's 13,600 square kilometres. Visit Rangitoto, noted for its harsh, volcanic landscape (strong-soled, non-slip shoes are advisable), or Motutapu, Motuihe and Waiheke, with good beaches and some 3,500 residents. Go for a nature walk on **Kawau Island**, home of a thriving colony of wallabies. Mansion House, once the residence of Governor Grey, also stands on the island.

For a change of pace, take the road through the wine-growing and orchard area of Henderson into the **Waitakere Ranges** (for details, contact the Arataki Visitor Information Centre, tel. 817 7134) and **Titirangi**. The route leads through lush, hilly suburbs. Stop off at vineyards on the way for a spot of wine-tasting.

Excursion to Coromandel

A beautiful area for back-packers and nature-lovers, the **Coromandel Peninsula** stretches out a jagged finger south-east of Auckland. It's wild in places, with plenty of opportunities for hunting, fishing and skin-diving. In the 19th century the region was exploited for kauri timber, gum and gold. Great areas of forest were destroyed, but some remain, providing a home for rare species

of frog, the North Island crow (*korako*), hundreds of kingfishers, and big seabird colonies on offshore islands. Semi-precious stones such as camelian, agate, chalcedony and jasper are washed down from the hills into creeks and mingle with the pebbles on the western beaches.

Many of the roads are difficult going for motorists, but there's a highway along the west coast to Coromandel settlement. Stop off at **Waihi**, where New Zealand's biggest gold strike was made in 1878. At **Thames** the old-timers can show you gold-mining relics and spin many a yarn. A few still work their claims, though real mining ceased in the 1920s. In **Coromandel** itself, 56 kilometres north of Thames, you'll find more tall tales and streets of colonial buildings – like something out of a Hollywood western.

If you explore this area on foot, watch out for disused mine-shafts concealed by vegetation. Make sure of your bush-survival techniques before taking on the great outdoors.

Northland

Northland extends from Auckland to Cape Reinga. Known as the 'Winterless North' because of its mild climate, the region has also been dubbed the 'Land of a Thousand Beaches'. Sheltered bays like Matapouri, Oakura and Doubtless Bay fringe the coast; so do dozens of coves (some of them accessible only by boat) and an almost unbroken series of beaches stretching from Pouto, on Kaipara Harbour, all the way north to the cape. Sporting opportunities abound: Ninety Mile Beach hosts the biggest surfcasting competition in the whole of the southern hemisphere. Game fishing is a major attraction and there's skin-diving, too, especially around Poor Knight Islands. Parts of the region are covered by thick rainforest, including concentrations of New Zealand's forest giant, the kauri tree.

Missionaries established stations in the Bay of Islands from 1814 onwards. Kororareka (now Russell) represented another aspect of Western culture. It was a brawling, bawdy, gun-toting centre for whaling and sealing, described by 19th-century seamen as the 'hell-hole of the Pacific'.

You can fly to the north, but you'll miss a lot. The fastest road is east via Waipu and Whangarei; but the west coast road, though rough in places, bisects Trounson

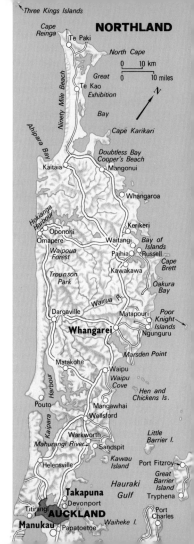

Park and Waipoua Forest, where the superb kauri trees are protected. A good compromise is to head north by way of Whangarei, returning via Opononi, Omapere and Dargaville.

Auckland to Whangarei

The quiet farming township of **Warkworth**, some 69 kilometres north of Auckland, stands alongside the picturesque Mahurangi River. To the east lies Sandspit, terminus for the ferries to Kawau Island (see p. 32). There are fine beaches at **Mangawhai**, further up the coast.

The little Scottish enclave of **Waipu** was founded by a group of Highlanders who moved first to Nova Scotia and then to Australia before arriving in New Zealand in 1853. Their leader, Norman McLeod, was a Calvinist minister whose fanaticism inspired both adoration and hatred. The Waipu House of Memories displays his portrait, as well as other pioneer memorabilia. On a hot day, make for **Waipu Cove**, one of the best beaches around.

Some 40,000 people call **Whangarei** home. It's the biggest town in the north, with an excellent deep-water harbour. The country's major oil refinery is situated at Marsden Point. Call in at the Clapham Clock Museum to hear the ticking and chiming of around 400 timepieces. At **Whangarei Falls** (off the road to Ngunguru) you can cool off in one of the three river pools.

Bay of Islands

Paihia makes a good base for excursions to the Bay of Islands. The town traces its history back to 1823, when the Reverend Henry Williams established New Zealand's third mission station here. The **Church of St Paul** (1926) stands as a memorial to the minister and his brother, Bishop William Williams. A plaque nearby marks the place where New Zealand's first printer, William Colenso, produced the New Testament in Maori.

The *Tui*, a three-masted barque moored at Waitangi Bridge, serves as a **Shipwreck Museum**. Here you'll see relics and treasures – including some Rothschild jewels – recovered from hundreds of New Zealand shipwrecks. Audio-visual exhibits illustrate Northland marine life. A pathway through mangrove and bush heads upstream to the impressive **Haruru Falls** (count on three hours).

Come what may, don't miss a **cruise** on the beautiful Bay of Islands, *the* thing to do in Paihia. It was Captain Cook who settled on the apt and simple name for this marine paradise studded with some 150 islands. 'Very uncommon and romantic', he said of them. The choice of launch trips includes a breakfast cruise, a lunchtime champagne cruise, a long run all the way to Cape Brett and Piercy Island, and the so-called Cream Trip, which originated in 1920 as a means of collecting products from farms scattered around the bay.

One notable point of interest in the Bay of Islands is **Marsden Cross**: this marks the spot where Samuel Marsden preached the first Christian sermon on December 25, 1814. **Moturua Island** provided shelter in 1772 for the French explorer Marion du Fresne who, along with 16 members of his crew, was killed (and eaten) by Maoris at Te Hue later that year. His lieutenant claimed the country for France, unaware that Cook had already scooped the pool for Britain. A monument donated by the French in 1972 commemorates the bicentenary of du Fresne's landing. As launchmasters round Cape Brett, passengers gasp at their prowess in negotiating the deceptive cleft known as the 'Hole in the Rock'.

Waitangi, 'Wailing Waters', is aptly named. For this is where the Maoris signed the controversial treaty of 1840 by which the British assumed sovereignty over New Zealand (see p. 20).

You can visit **Treaty House**, built in 1833 for the British Resident James Busby, now a museum. A flagstaff in front of the house marks the spot where the treaty was signed. A commemoration ceremony is held here every year on February 6. A Maori **meeting-house** *(whare runanga)*, built for the centennial celebrations in 1940, stands nearby. Typically, a meeting-house contains carvings made by one tribe only, but this impressive building, representing all the Maori people, houses outstanding **carvings** from many different tribes. The standing figure *(tekoteko)* at the apex of the roof represents the ancestors of the Maoris who sailed from Polynesia centuries ago. Inside, a series of wall slabs *(poupou)* illustrates regional styles of carving.

A meeting-house has a symbolic human form: the apex of the roof serves as the head, the **35** ridgepole as the backbone, the bargeboards as arms, the rafters as ribs and the space inside as the chest and belly. The spectacular war canoe in the adjacent canoe-house was also made for the centenary and can carry 150 men. Nearby, Mt Bledisloe affords fine views of the Bay of Islands.

Regular ferry services and road connections link Paihia to **Russell**, across the bay. This sleepy little settlement once had a far from sleepy reputation. Grog and girls were the main attractions in the days when it was a rumbustious whaling port known by the Maori name Kororareka. The Duke of Marlborough Hotel on the waterfront, rebuilt several times, lays claim to the oldest liquor licence in the country. The handsome kauriwood Police Station was built in 1870, well after the fire which destroyed most of the town's old buildings.

Pompallier House incorporates part of the original *pisé* (mud, clay and ash) building constructed for the French Catholic Bishop of the South-West Pacific, Jean-Baptiste Pompallier; he installed the mission's printing

Lovely Bay of Islands, site of the
36 *first permanent settlement.*

presses here. The Bungalow, next door, was home to James Clendon, the first American Consul.

Visit **Christ Church** (1836), the oldest surviving church in the country. The evolutionist Charles Darwin contributed money for its construction. The **Captain Cook Memorial Museum** (in York Street) has a replica of Cook's barque, *Endeavour,* and mementoes of bad old Kororareka.

From **Flagstaff (Maiki) Hill** there is a fine view of the Bay of Islands. The hill has seen a succession of flagpoles rise and fall. The first was chopped down in 1844 by an influential Northland chief, Hone Heke. The first Maori to sign the Treaty of Waitangi, he had become wary of British land interests and irritated that dues from visiting ships which had once gone to him were now collected by the government. When the flagpole was re-erected, he axed it a second time. Four times in all he laid low this symbol of British power; then he attacked Kororareka township itself. A chance spark exploded the powder magazine, and the 'vile hole' (as a contemporary dubbed

Maori history comes very vividly alive in carvings at Waitangi.

the settlement) went up in smoke. When you visit the site of the flagpole you may or may not see one standing: it's still as controversial an issue as the Treaty of Waitangi itself.

Among the walks in the area, try one that's different – through the **Waitangi Mangrove Forest**, where you'll see mangrove trees 9 metres high. The salt swamp where they thrive supports all manner of fish and bird life. Take binoculars to observe the oyster-catchers, pied stilts and white-fronted herons, among others. All the while you'll be aware of a strange clicking – made by the elongated claws of the shrimps.

When choosing among sightseeing possibilities around the Bay of Islands, opt for **Kerikeri**. The still water of the Kerikeri Basin, the white-masted boats and dark, crowding bush give an idea of the magic and romance of old New Zealand. Overlooking the basin is **Kemp House**, the oldest building in New Zealand, completed in 1822. From 1832 until 1974 it sheltered the Kemp family, descendants of the Anglican lay missionary James Kemp and his wife, Charlotte.

The nearby **Stone Store** did double duty in 1832 as a shop and

> **Journey to the Underworld**
> The Maoris knew Ninety Mile Beach as Te-Oneroa-a-Tohe. It was tapu, sa-
> cred ground, the place frequented by the spirits of the dead on their journey
> to the spirit land. At Te Arai rock they left remembrances of their earthly
> home – a bunch of raupo reeds if they had lived near swampland, seaside
> grass if they came from the coast. At Twilight Beach they went inland to
> drink from a stream called 'Water of the Underworld'. Then they continued
> to an ancient pohutukawa tree, supposedly the gnarled giant that still clings
> to the cliffs below the lighthouse. The twisted, exposed roots served as a
> staircase to the ocean depths. The spirits emerged briefly at Ohau Island in
> the Three Kings for a last glimpse of Aotearoa before making their way to the
> mystical Maori homeland, far away Hawaiki.

a refuge for missionaries. Nowadays a museum occupies the floor
above the shop. **Rewa's Village**
up the hill is a *kainga* (unfortified
Maori village), which has been
reconstructed in authentic pre-
European style. At the heart of a
fruit-growing area, Kerikeri has
an abundance of orange, mandarin, kiwifruit and tamarillo
trees. You can hop on a miniature
train for an orchard tour.

A visit to **Wairoa sheep and
cattle station** near Paihia offers
scenic touring and an inside look
at farming. Other recommended
trips include the Ngawha Mineral
Springs, for sufferers of rheuma-
tism and arthritis, Puketi Kauri
Forest (19 kilometres north-west
of Kerikeri), Waimate for another
mission house (1831), and, when
the weather's good, Whangaroa,
Mangonui and Cooper's Beach.

Cape Reinga

Cape Reinga falls 5 kilometres
short of being the country's most
northerly point (that title belongs
to Surville Cliffs). Depending on
the tides, you can bowl along
hard sand to Cape Reinga lighthouse (116 kilometres up from
Kaitaia) or take the inland road
and return over the sand. Since
the salt is tough on cars (four-
wheel-drive vehicles are recommended), you may prefer to take
a coach tour. You'll see the great
arc of **Ninety Mile Beach**, so impressive that you won't think of
questioning the length – which is
actually only 60 miles. The vast
ocean walls you in on one side,
on the other side are pale, storm-
fingered dunes. Sometimes it's so
windy at the cape you can hardly
stand up straight. Black rocks and
screaming seagulls mark the end

of the land. Rippling into the distance is the line where the Tasman Sea meets the Pacific Ocean. Far out, barely visible, lie the Three Kings Islands.

The West Coast

The coastal route will take you through **Opononi**, a tiny settlement famous as the home of Opo, an extraordinary dolphin who visited the beach regularly for one brief summer in 1955. Opo cavorted with the children and played hide and seek with swimmers – until he was killed accidentally by fishermen using illegal charges of dynamite.

Waipoua Forest is a vestige of the kauri thickets that once covered much of Northland. The kauri *(Agathis australis)* grows slowly to a great height and lives for well over a thousand years. Indiscriminate felling by early settlers wiped out large areas. Quantities were exported for ships' spars. You'll be impressed by the grandeur of these majestic trees in their cool forest setting, and the huge colonies of bird and insect life they support. The most venerable trees are signposted. Look out for Te Matua Ngahere (Father of the Forest), which is 2,000 years old, and the younger

Tane Mahuta (God of the Forest), which is a mere 1,200.

Dargaville, south of Trounson Park (where there are more fine kauri trees), used to be a thriving centre for timber and gum. Many Yugoslav immigrants worked in the gum fields; the resin, which they found in the ground or bled from the trees, was used in the manufacture of hard varnish. Their descendants

Once prized for ships' masts, in Northland kauri is king.

still live here. Exhibits of local interest fill the **Northern Wairoa Maori, Maritime and Pioneer Museum** (open in the afternoons only). At Matakohe, 50 kilometres south, the **Otamatea Kauri and Pioneer Museum** (signposted) will tell you all there is to know about the kauri.

Central North Island

Most visitors to New Zealand head out of Auckland, down the southern motorway and through Hamilton, to Waitomo Caves and the Rotorua thermal area.

On the way, you will pass through **Ngaruawahia**, the former centre of the Maori King Movement (see p. 20). Turangawaewae Maori Village is the official residence of the reigning Maori monarch, to whom a number of tribes swear allegiance and government representatives offer their respects on ceremonial occasions. The monarch's role has considerable social and cultural significance. On Regatta Day, a moveable date in March, the village is open to the public and there are canoe races on the river.

The city of **Hamilton** (population 170,000) is the rapidly expanding capital of a rich dairy-farming and agricultural region. The town began life as a British military settlement on the banks of the Waikato River. Pleasant as it is, with lovely suburban gardens and parks along the river, attractions are limited. Hilldale Zoo might make a break for the children; the Waikato Art Museum houses Maori artefacts; and there are some riverside walks.

Otorohanga, some 60 kilometres south, has the largest walk-through **aviary** in Australasia. If you missed the kiwis in Auckland, catch up with them here in the Nocturnal House.

Waitomo Caves

Occasional outcrops of stratified limestone mark the approach to Waitomo. A network of caves and underground galleries honeycombs the area. There are three caves open to the public. Guides accompany all tours and provide an excellent commentary.

A short walk through the bush takes you to **Ruakuri Cave**, said to be named after a pack of wild dogs *(kuri)* who made life impossible in these parts. The Maori chief who killed them is buried in a small cave above the entrance. The place was *tapu* until fairly recently. In **Aranui Cave**, named after its Maori discoverer, sophisticated lighting transforms the stalactites and stalagmites into floating pillars of cloud and fire.

Waitomo Cave itself – the name means 'Water Hole' – is a series of chambers and galleries, penetrated by the Waitomo River, which flows into the hillside here. The first European explorer entered by raft and was dazzled,

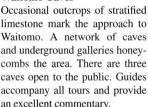

43

as every other visitor has been, by the magical beauty of the **Glow-worm Grotto**. Today you still view the grotto from a boat, pulled across the river by a fixed wire. Visitors are warned to keep complete silence: the slightest sound would dim the brilliance of the thousands of bluish lights that illumine the darkness and reflect in the inky water below.

The glow-worms in New Zealand are larvae of a mosquito-like fly (*Arachnocampa luminosa*), quite unrelated to the European glow-worm beetle and seldom found elsewhere. With tail-light glimmering, the larva swings to and fro in a kind of gossamer hammock, letting down sticky threads to catch midges which breed in the water. The adult fly is rarely seen. In spite of its ethereal appearance, the larva is not very discriminating and often consumes its own parents.

For more speleological insights, visit the **Waitomo Caves Museum** or have a go at **'adventure caving'**. You'll need warm clothes and sturdy footwear; everything else is provided. The Tourist Hotel Corporation (THC) hotel at Waitomo can supply you with all the information about this and other sightseeing trips.

Rotorua

'Sulphur City' is a popular name for Rotorua – you'll notice the smell as soon as you draw near. There's thermal activity throughout much of New Zealand – above all in the Rotorua area, a major safety valve for various subterranean upheavals. Steam drifts up from drains and private gardens, and the golf course even has thermal hazards.

The people of Rotorua have harnessed some of this natural energy for central heating. The same goes for swimming pools: many houses and most motels have one. Concrete 'steam boxes' in suburban gardens are used for preparing outdoor feasts.

Rotorua enjoys a delightful situation: cool and sunny in winter, hot and dry in summer. And it's growing at a tremendous rate. The present population is nearing 50,000. In addition to all the attributes of Old Nick's kitchen, the city offers access to glorious lakes and streams abounding in trout, as well as nature walks through the surrounding bush, man-made forests and rewarding glimpses into Maori culture.

Ohinemutu Maori Village lies on the shore of Lake Rotorua. Inoffensive steam vents and

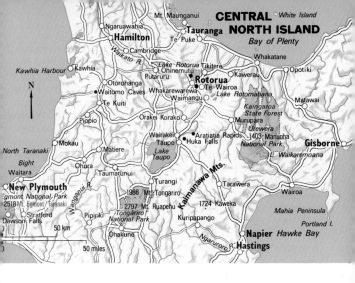

Central North Island map showing Bay of Plenty, White Island, Mt Maunganui, Tauranga, Te Puke, Whakatane, Opotiki, Ngaruawahia, Hamilton, Cambridge, Kawhia Harbour, Kawhia, Waikato R., Lake Rotorua, Tikitere, Kawerau, Otorohanga, Putaruru, Ohinemutu, Rotorua, Te Wairoa, Matawai, Waitomo Caves, Whakarewarewa, Te Kuiti, Waimangu, Lake Rotomahana, Piopio, Orakei Korako, Kaingaroa State Forest, Murupara, Urewera, Mokau, Wairakei, Aratiatia Rapids, Manuoha 1403, National Park, Gisborne, North Taranaki Bight, Matiere, Taupo, Huka Falls, L. Waikaremoana, Ohura, Lake Taupo, New Plymouth, Egmont National Park, 2518 Mt. Egmont/Taranaki, Dawson Falls, Stratford, Taumarunui, Turangi, Tarawera, Wairoa, Pipiriki, 1986 Mt. Tongariro, 2797 Mt. Ruapehu, 1724 Kaweka, Mahia Peninsula, Portland I., Tongariro National Park, Kuripapango, Ohakune, Napier, Hawke Bay, Hastings, Wanganui R., Kaimanawa Mts., Ngaruroro R. Scale 50 km / 50 miles. N compass.

boiling pools hiss and bubble away between the buildings. **St Faith's Anglican Church**, right on the lake's edge, should be visited for its remarkable pews, pulpit and altar enriched with traditional Maori carving. Etched into the chancel window is a depiction of Christ wearing the feathered cloak of a Maori chief, placed so that the figure appears to be walking on water. Services here are held in Maori, and the singing is superlative. Opposite the church stands **Tamatekapua meeting-house**, named after the captain of the Arawa canoe from whose occupants the members of the Arawa tribe claims descent. Nearby, **Kuirau Domain** offers hot vents and pools, thermal foot baths, and a miniature train for the children. **Government Gardens**, known to the Maoris as Whangapiro ('Place of Evil Odours') is immaculately maintained. Amid the gardens stands a wonderful old building, **Tudor Towers** (1907), an Edwardian gesture to Elizabethan architecture. Local people still call it the 'Bath House', in memory of the fashionable spa centre that used to operate here. Inside you'll find a museum and art gallery. You can take a plunge in the tepid twin swimming-pools called the Blue Baths, or soak in the therapeutic Polynesian Pools at the eastern end of Hinemoa Street. **Sulphur Point**, behind Tudor Towers, is a lakeside bathing spot in sight of Mokoia Island.

The best-known thermal area lies just outside town at **Whaka-irewarewa**. The local people call it 'Whaka'. First you come to a small Maori village, approached over a bridge, where generations of little boys have dived for coins. Great waves of hydrogen sulphide waft in the air, which smells like rotten eggs. Once you could catch trout in the Whaka stream and lower them straight into a hot pool to cook, but nearby timber milling has put paid to this forerunner to fast food.

Geyser Flat features seven active geysers, but the star is **Pohutu** (Maori for 'splash'), which erupts several times a day on average and can gush to over 30 metres. Pools and mud-pots all bubble pungently away, some

Rotorua's Tudor Towers museum and relaxing spa waters.

plopping like porridge, some weirdly coloured. Don't ever stray off the paths in the hope of getting a better view. The ground is a mere crust in places. The same applies to all thermal areas: they are safe as long as you take the warning signs seriously.

Visit **Rotowhio model village** to see what a pre-European fortified *pa* looked like. The gateway is carved with the embracing figures of the legendary lovers, Hinemoa and Tutanekai. Maori carvers can be seen at work in the nearby **Arts and Crafts Institute**. Traditions are rigorously passed from old to young.

The Waimangu-Tarawera trip is one of the best and most comprehensive thermal excursions. A little walking is involved; but you can arrange transport to avoid it, and provision can be made for visitors in wheelchairs.

The **Waimangu** thermal valley was created in 1886 when Mt Tarawera suddenly exploded. Flashes of fire were seen as far away as Auckland and detonations were heard in Christchurch, 650 kilometres south. Ash blackened the air, streams of mud and lava engulfed Maori dwellings and European houses. Destroyed in the eruption were the Pink and

White Terraces, one of the great thermal wonders of the world.

Tarawera is still haunted by the legend of the ghost canoe. Eleven days before the eruption a 110-year-old Maori priest *(to-*

hunga) reported sighting a huge

Pohutu geyser shows off in style at Whaka thermal reserve.

war canoe paddling across Lake Tarawera. The Maoris in the area took it as an omen of impending tragedy. In addition, two parties of Europeans claimed that they had seen a phantom canoe. Fact or fiction, the Tarawera area is so sensationally savage that even the most sceptical tourists tend to agree that much of it should be regarded as *tapu*.

The Waimangu trip takes in a walk through places of thermal interest to **Lake Rotomahana**, followed by a launch trip across the lake, a short walk to **Lake Tarawera**, a second cruise, and a visit to **Te Wairoa**, a buried village that is the New Zealand equivalent of Pompeii. Ask in the souvenir shop here and they'll show you a superb carving of that phantom canoe. You return via the **Blue and Green Lakes**.

You may feel yourself on another planet at **Tikitere**, also known as 'Hell's Gate'. Even the waterfall is steaming. George Bernard Shaw said he wished he'd never seen it: 'It reminds me too vividly of the fate theologians have promised me', he remarked.

A number of **trout springs** are set in attractive parklands. Rainbow Springs has a fern walk; Fairy Springs, tinted an unbelievable shade of turquoise, sports its own waterfall; Taniwha Springs marks the site of an old Maori village; Paradise Valley has a small zoo; and Hamurana, reached through a stand of Californian redwoods, pours out millions of litres of water an hour. In all these places the trout swim around freely and you can feed them by hand. If you want to try some fishing, call in at the Visitor Information Centre, 67 Fenton Street, Rotorua (see p. 92).

Don't leave without a visit to the **Agrodome** at Ngongotaha, on the northern outskirts of Rotorua. The daily shows are a great way of finding out more about New Zealand's sheep. Afterwards, woolly aristocrats condescend to being petted and photographed.

Mt Ngongotaha has a cable car to the restaurant at the summit, where you can enjoy the fabulous views of the city and lake; try the luge for a fast descent.

Hongi's Track, the verdant forest road joining Lakes Rotoiti and Rotoehu, is named after the Northland chief, Hongi Hika, who portaged canoes through here to wage war against the local tribe. A signposted tree, commemorates the spot where a famous chieftainess, Hinehopu, met her husband 400 years ago. Offer a fern frond, murmur a few respectful words (the tree is *tapu*), circle it, and you'll have a safe journey. **49**

When the people of Rotorua yearn for sea and sand, they usually drive to **Ocean Beach** at Mt Maunganui on the east coast, one of the best in the country. Offshore there are game fish for the taking around Mayor and Potiti islands. A ferry service links 'the Mount' to the harbour town of **Tauranga**.

Evening entertainment in Rotorua runs the gamut from concerts to splendid Maori feasts.

Wairakei

Wairakei (74 kilometres south of Rotorua) is right in the centre of an active volcanic zone that extends some 241 kilometres from Mt Ruapehu through Taupo and Rotorua to White Island, a smoking volcano in the Bay of Plenty. Anyone who is interested in thermal engineering will find this area fascinating, while anglers will enjoy fishing in the Waikato River pools and in Lake Taupo.

The road from Rotorua to Wairakei, running south from Whakarewarewa, provides good views of **Rainbow Mountain** (just past the Waimangu turnoff). The rock-face is tinted a delicate pink, beige and cream. Botanists delight in the area for its abundance of rare plants.

Watch out for the signposts to **Waiotapu**, the site of Lady Knox Geyser and a Champagne Pool (toss a handful of sand in to make it fizz). On a good day you can see the mountains of Tongariro National Park floating in the distance. You can take a boat trip across the Waikato River to the silica terraces at **Orakei Korako**. Some evening tours include a swim in a hot pool. To the east is the vast **Kaingaroa State Forest** (150,000 hectares), much of it planted with radiata pine during the Depression of the 1930s.

Once you are out of the forest, watch for a turnoff to **Aratiatia Rapids**. The dam of the hydroelectric station – one of several on the Waikato River – opens at 10am, noon and 2pm, and also at 4.0 pm in summer, so tourists can witness the great rush of water. The Wairakei geothermal project is the second largest of its kind in the world (the biggest is in Italy). The system taps an underground water supply heated by hot or even molten rock. Steam is obtained by drilling. The process is as complicated as the complex is

Crimson blossoms and smoking mountains – the New Zealand landscape is full of surprises.

awesome: great clouds of vapour roll across the landscape. Visit the public lookout for a bird's eye view of the steam valley.

Don't miss the **Huka Falls**, 4 kilometres south on the road to Taupo. The Waikato River leaps a ledge into a foaming pool, and a jet-boat ride gives an awesome view of the falls from their base. **Craters of the Moon** (almost opposite) is another thermal area. This one's pretty scary, especially since it's relatively unvisited. Danger limits are clearly marked.

Taupo

The name is synonymous with angling. New Zealand's largest lake covers 616 square kilometres and gives rise to its longest river, the Waikato (354 km). Every year an incredible 700 tonnes of trout are taken from Taupo's waters.

Summer is the peak season, when the trout are fat from feasting on green beetle, but dedicated anglers prefer the spawning season in autumn and winter. No angler can call himself 'compleat' if he hasn't cast a fly into the **Tongariro River**, known to fishing enthusiasts all around the world. The Taupo Information Centre in Tongariro Street or the THC Hotel, Tokaanu, will pro-

vide fishermen with information and arrange helicopter transport to bushland streams and pools.

You will enjoy the peaceful atmosphere of the town of **Taupo** with its temperate climate and clear, blue lake. If you tire of fishing, there's swimming, water-skiing and boating. You can visit Cherry Island wildlife park, the small Regional Museum in Story Place, and the Honey Centre, where glass hives bare the private lives of the bees. Or opt for the fairly easy two-hour walk to the top of Mt Tauhara.

Tongariro National Park

Three great volcanic peaks dominate Tongariro National Park, a short drive south of Taupo. Considered guardian deities by the Maoris, they were presented to the nation in 1887 by the paramount chief of the area in an act of generous confidence. Now they constitute the North Island's big ski playground. When things get going in Vulcan's workshop, you can listen to the bangs and fireworks from one active volcano while you skim (perhaps rather faster than usual!) down the slopes of another.

You'll learn to recognize the names of the three mighty peaks

The delicate kiwifruit – now one of New Zealand's major exports.

before you can pronounce them: **Mt Ruapehu**, with the gracious old Grand Chateau Hotel; **Mt Tongariro**, officially dormant but still steaming: and **Mt Ngauruhoe**, the country's most tirelessly vociferous volcano, which last hit the headlines back in 1945 when it gushed some sensational fountains of molten lava. No need for nerves: all activity is constantly monitored.

Main ski-fields, all of them on Mt Ruapehu, are at Whakapapa (Chateau); Turoa, south-west on the mountain; and Tukino, to the east. There are conditions to suit all skiers, from gentle nursery slopes to the national downhill course. The park offers plenty of walks and climbing. It also has

some excellent accommodation in a system of huts, as well as camping, motels and the European-style Chateau itself. Find out all about it at Park Headquarters, near the Chateau, or write to the Chief Ranger, Park Headquarters, Mt Ruapehu. Hunting permits are available.

East Cape and Hawke's Bay

Gloriously sunny and very beautiful in parts, this area is little known to overseas visitors. The 344-kilometre coastal route from Opotiki to Gisborne offers good beaches and pleasant scenery. **Gisborne**, incidentally, has the honour of being the first town in the world to behold the new day, because of its proximity to the International Date Line.

Urewera National Park, inland from Gisborne in the rugged Urewera Range, is a magnificent expanse of primeval forest. Exceptional hunting and hiking can be enjoyed in this area, as well as some excellent fishing in **Lake Waikaremoana** ('Sea of Shining Water') – a sublime expanse of azure in the midst of the forest.

Hawke's Bay province, the fruit bowl of New Zealand, is wealthy, welcoming and warm – you can count on day after day of blue skies and sunshine. The twin cities of Napier and Hastings are friendly rivals for the title of top town. In 1931 the district suffered a disastrous earthquake. Both cities were reduced to rubble, and Napier was swept by fire. Some 4,000 hectares of seabed were raised in the quake.

The **Napier** of today, with its Marine Parade of Norfolk pines, has all been rebuilt. The town's

Autumn gilds the trees; spring brings new life to the gannets.

older residents still recall the terrible ten days of violent tremors that changed the face of the landscape, split roads into fissures, swallowed vehicles and people, crumbled cliffs and toppled buildings. The tremors were recorded as far away as India and Great Britain. The host of holiday attractions in Napier's Marine Parade include **Marineland**, with excellent seal and dolphin shows, and a big aquarium. **55**

Hastings is one of several important wine-producing centres in this area, so you'll have plenty of opportunities for tasting.

Don't miss the **gannet sanctuary** at Cape Kidnappers: drive the 21 kilometres to Clifton Domain, then walk the remaining 8 kilometres to the world's only known mainland gannet colony. Coach tours are also available. Summer months are the time to see some 15,000 of these superb seabirds, more streamlined than any aircraft, with snowy plumage, distinctive yellow heads and strong black-tipped pinions. Eggs are laid in October and November. Four months later the birds set off on their annual migration to Australia. The chicks reside there for four years, then return to breed.

Taranaki

Long ago, according to Maori legend, Mt Taranaki lived happily with the other volcanoes in the centre of the North Island. One day, however, Mt Tongariro discovered that Taranaki was paying court to his wife, a charming lady volcano near Lake Taupo. In the battle that ensued, Taranaki was forced to flee to the west, gouging out the Wanganui River as he went, before retreating north, whence he continues to glare at his old rival.

Nowadays Taranaki, officially known as **Mt Egmont/Taranaki**, rises from bright green farmland, a solitary, snowcapped peak, its lower slopes thickly forested. The mountain offers some good skiing, and you can climb it in a day. But don't attempt the ascent without a guide; in spite of its beauty, the mountain can be deadly.

Egmont/Taranaki serves as a dramatic backdrop for the town of **New Plymouth**. Take a daytime stroll to view the gardens of **Pukekura Park**, one of the finest in the country, and visit again at night to see the floodlit waterfall. Further botanical delights await you at the **Pukeiti Rhododendron Trust** (29 kilometres out of town on the Upper Carrington Road), noted for the stunning beauty of its rhododendrons and azaleas. The **Taranaki Museum** houses a fine collection of Maori stone sculpture, and the **Govett-Brewster Art Gallery** specializes in contemporary Pacific art.

Wanganui

Set at the mouth of the Wanganui River, the town of Wanganui has an excellent **museum** with some awe-inspiring skeletons of *moas*, the huge birds that became extinct in pre-European times. Go up in the Durie Hill elevator for a splendid view of the town. **Putiki Church** (1937) contains some marvellous Maori carvings.

The **river** is undoubtedly the main attraction here. In late summer it's the scene of motorboat regattas. Try one of the jet-boat tours. A New Zealand invention, perfect for shallow rapids, these craft move by drawing in water and expelling it. Gentler launch and canoe excursions are available, too. The loveliest reaches of the river lie 30 kilometres or so above **Pipiriki**.

Wellington

There's an assurance and an international flair to Wellington. The capital of New Zealand has a resident population of only 330,000, yet it's every inch a city. Seen from the hill-encircled harbour it looks a little like Hong Kong and a lot like San Francisco. Wellingtonians find Aucklanders brash; and Aucklanders regard Wellingtonians as a club of toffee-nosed civil servants. But each secretly admires the other. It's an ancient rivalry – for Wellington replaced Auckland as the capital in 1865.

Wellington is nicknamed the 'Windy City' – and that's not an

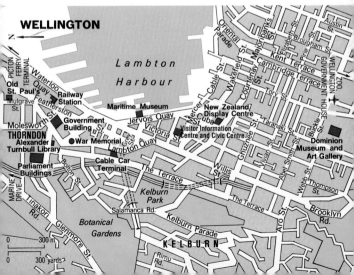

exaggeration, the wind here can knock you clean off your feet. In fact, Wellingtonians should make the world's best mountaineers. They live perched up in the hills around the downtown area and climb innumerable steps to get home; dozens of winding alleys and stairways lead up to the colonial houses. Down in the business district, though, old Wellington is

Highrise buildings are a striking feature of the Wellington skyline.

disappearing. The glass and concrete invasion of soaring modern buildings is a cause of regret for many who loved the higgledy-piggledy character of the place.

You can go for a city tour on one of Wellington's red buses, boarding at the Visitor Information Centre next to the Central Library, in the Wellington City Council Civic Centre on Victoria Street. Private companies operate tours of the city, too. Or you may prefer to walk around the major

points of interest on your own, which takes about four hours.

Wellington's main commercial street, **Lambton Quay**, used to run along the waterfront, but reclamation has pushed the land out. A plaque in the pavement at Stewart Dawson's Corner marks the old shoreline. Take the funicular (from Cable Car Lane, opposite Grey Street) up to Kelburn to enjoy the views of the inner harbour and central city. Paths to the right of the terminal lead to the

Lady Norwood Rose Garden and Begonia House.

The National Library building in Molesworth Street is the home of the **Alexander Turnbull Library**, with its fine collection of books, manuscripts, photographs and paintings relating to New Zealand. The exhibition gallery is well worth a visit. Weekdays you can join a tour of the building.

Three buildings make up the **Parliament complex** (entrance in Molesworth Street). Its austere main building (1922) loses out to the Neo-Gothic General Assembly Library (1897), whose arches and spires bring a beguiling hint of frivolity to the seat of national government. The latest addition is an impressive domed structure known as 'the Beehive'. In front of the complex stands a lofty statue of the much-loved prime minister Richard John Seddon, whose proudest claim was: 'I am a humanist'. Tours of the Library and main building have been temporarily suspended while renovation work is in progress.

The design of old **St Paul's** in Mulgrave Street (1864) adapted the early Gothic style to meet the requirements of a wooden building. The architect-vicar, Frederick Thatcher, was responsible for **59** many fine churches throughout New Zealand, and St Paul's is probably the best. The church's carved pulpit was presented by Seddon's widow.

The old **Government Building** (1876) at the north end of Lambton Quay is the second largest wooden building in the world, constructed almost entirely of native timber. The cost so far exceeded estimates that the government of the day decided discretion was the better part of valour, and there was no official inauguration. A pleasant little **Maritime Museum** on Jervois Quay displays historic paintings, photographs and charts.

The **National Museum and Art Gallery** (in Buckle Street), recognizable by the War Memorial Carillon tower, has a good Maori section. Here, too, is the

The painted houses and weaving streets contribute to Wellington's enduring charm.

collection of botanical specimens assembled by Captain Cook's naturalists, and the figurehead of the *Resolution*, the ship in which Cook made his second and third voyages to New Zealand. The Art Gallery boasts an interesting range of works, including early New Zealand paintings and some Rembrandts and Dürers.

Going along **Marine Drive**, which starts at Oriental Bay, you will see an enormous variety of coastline, from the sand beaches of chic suburbia to jagged rocks and grey, rolling sea. At Oriental Bay itself make a detour to the **Mt Victoria lookout** (signposted), for superb city and harbour views. The stone memorial commemorates the American Antarctic explorer Rear Admiral Byrd (1887–1957), who made New Zealand the starting point for his expeditions and achieved the first flight over the South Pole.

Newtown Park Zoo, 4 kilometres out of town, has a kiwi house and a lively collection of native and exotic animals.

From Wellington, inter-island passenger and car ferries head across Cook Strait to delightful, drowsy, little Picton – a suitably picturesque prelude to the scenic wonders of the South Island.

The South Island

Noble landscapes and friendly people typify the South Island. Often you'll hear a warm burr in the voices, an inheritance from early Scottish settlers. The main city is Christchurch.

To the North lie the Marlborough Sounds, a jumble of inlets, islands and peninsulas that, from the air, look like an abandoned jigsaw puzzle. The Southern Alps run almost the length of the island in a snowcapped ridge. To the west forests flourish, watered by constant downpours – unleashed as clouds mount abruptly into the cold air of the mountains. To the east stretch wide plains built up by rivers carrying shingle from the Alps. South-west is the spectacular beauty of Fiordland, so wild and remote that only experienced hikers penetrate far into its virgin bushland. Finally, to the south, there's New Zealand's third major land-mass, Stewart Island. From this haven of beach and forest you can at times see the *aurora australis* staining the sky like a giant neon display advertising the South Pole. The phenomenon inspired the Maori's poetic name for Stewart Island: Rakiura or 'Heavenly Glow.'

Nelson and Marlborough

Two major inlets, Queen Charlotte Sound and Pelorus Sound, penetrate the northernmost part of the South Island. The inter-island ferry crosses the rough water of Cook Strait and passes close to The Brothers, a group of barren islands that are home to the rare tuatara, only surviving member of the 'beak-headed' reptile family that became extinct over 100 million years ago. Look out for dolphins riding the ship's bow wave – including the small, rare Hectors dolphin found only off New Zealand. Then the ferry turns into Tory Channel and continues up Queen Charlotte Sound to the deepwater port of **Picton**.

The people of Picton firmly believe that their town is the real centre of New Zealand, though there are only 3,500 permanent residents. In summer the population swells considerably, for Picton is the hub of the popular Marlborough Sounds area.

Among Picton's sights are the Smith Memorial Museum, with relics of the harsh old whaling days, and two venerable sailing ships moored close to the town: *The Echo*, beached in Picton Harbour, the last sail trading vessel in New Zealand; and the *Edwin Fox* in Shakespeare Bay, one of the oldest sailing ships in existence, built as a tea clipper in 1843. In the Crimean War it carried Florence Nightingale as a passenger. Local walks include a night-time ramble from Garden Terrace to Humphrey's Dam, with a myriad glow-worms for lighting.

Marlborough Sounds

Although there are coach trips and 'flightseeing' for an overall view, the Sounds are best explored by boat. Picton offers an astonishing variety of vessels for hire, from charter launches to water taxis. Historic spots in the Sounds include **Ship Cove**, visited five times by Captain Cook, **Motuara Island**, where he raised the British flag, and **French Pass**, a dangerous stretch of water first navigated in colonial times by the Frenchman Dumont d'Urville – who gave his name to the large island lying offshore. John Guard's whaling station on **Te Awaiti Bay** (Tory Channel), founded in 1827, is said to have been the first European settlement on the South Island, and John's wife, the first white woman to live there.

Main water trips pass through Queen Charlotte's Grove Arm to **Double Cove**, where there's a

twice-daily feast for tame snapper. The Queen Charlotte Sound mail run varies its route from day to day in order to serve every outlying household, and the Pelorus Sound jaunt sets off four times a week from Havelock, at the head of Pelorus Sound. For some outstanding fishing (not allowed near the tame snapper grounds), you can arrange to be dropped off at certain points and picked up again later in the day; Pelorus and Kenepuru sounds are recommended. In addition to the snapper (some over 8kg), there are also blue and red cod, terakihi, tuna, kahawai (sea trout,) groper *(hapuka)*, garfish and butterfish, depending on where and how you drop your line.

The coastal area that runs from the Sounds to south of **Kaikoura** enjoys a reputation for surf fishing. Divers can find crayfish at Port Underwood, Titirangi (100 km from Picton), Tory Channel and D'Urville Island, or dive to wrecks, particularly near Cape Jackson and south of D'Urville. Fish abound in most rivers, but anglers favour the Wairau, Awatere and Clarence for salmon and the Pelorus and Wairau rivers and Spring Creek for trout. Vernon Lagoons (to the south-east of

Blenheim) and Para Swamp are celebrated for duck-shooting (in season) and bird-watching.

Blenheim, just 29 kilometres south of Picton, claims to be the sunniest spot in New Zealand, so not surprisingly there are lots of vineyards round about. However,

Calm stretches of water await visitors to Marlborough Sounds.

it was once so marshy that it was known as Beavertown, and the beaver is still the town's emblem. It's bigger than Picton (with a population of 17,500) and, like it, a centre for visiting the region. Pause at Brayshaw Museum Park to see a replica of old Beaver-

town and an interesting collection of vintage farm machinery.

Although it has only 300 inhabitants, the tiny township of

Havelock (which can claim the distinction of being the birthplace of Dr William Pickering, the space scientist in charge of the first moon landing) is quietly self-assured. It lies 43 kilometres from Blenheim, but the most enjoyable way of getting here is from Picton (38 kilometres), taking the picturesque Grove Track (Queen Charlotte Drive). Be sure to sample the delicious scallops brought in by the local fishing fleet and the equally good mussels farmed in the Sounds. In the Havelock Museum you can see souvenirs of the town's beginnings as a timber-milling centre. Havelock, too, has a night-time glow-worm walk. Outings available are similar to those from Picton (see p.62).

In and Around Nelson City

Glorious beaches, golden sunshine and spectacular sunsets, that's the town of **Nelson** (population 33,000). Situated on Tasman Bay, Nelson also lies close to some fine national parks.

Christ Church Cathedral, set in lovely grounds, dominates the city. Also well worth attention are the Nelson Provincial Museum and Isel House, a stone homestead, nearby. Broadgreen,

designed on the lines of a Devon farmhouse, is another fine old residence. Queen's Gardens offer a pleasant surround to the Suter Art Gallery; look for the painting of Ship's Cove by Cook's official artist (third voyage), James Webber. South Street boasts many colonial houses, several of which have been turned into galleries featuring contemporary pottery fashioned from local clay. For a view over the whole city and Tasman Bay, climb Botanical Hill. You look down on the playing field where the country's first rugby match took place in 1870 – a momentous date in Kiwi history. Nelson's best beach, Tahunanui, is only 5 kilometres from the town centre.

Many people use Nelson as their base for excursions into the nearby national parks. Walk the Heaphy Track in **North-West Nelson State Forest**, or explore the 57,000 hectares of **Nelson Lakes National Park**. Picnic spots abound around Lakes Rotoiti and Rotoroa, surrounded by beautiful red, silver and black beech forests and rich in rare plants. **Abel Tasman National Park**, to the north-west, offers prime opportunities for camping, boating, swimming and hiking.

To reach the main point of entry, you pass through the fruit-growing district of Motueka and take the road leading to Takaka.

Bus tours depart from Motueka for **Takaka Hill** (better known as Marble Mountain) and the **Ngarua Marble Caves**. Some 35 kilometres before Takaka, the landscape becomes increasingly surrealistic as spectral trees alternate with pitted stone. Weathered outcrops thrusting through bracken and tussock cover large areas of Takaka Hill. Most quarrying is done at Kairuru. The marble here varies in quality, and the colour ranges from grey to pink. Marble Mountain itself is almost hollow – it's a whole labyrinth of sinkholes and tunnels formed by the acid content of the water which drips into it. **Harwoods Hole**, the deepest sinkhole in the country (a 45-minute walk from the end of the Canaan Road), plunges 370 metres into the mountain's heart.

The road snakes tortuously over Marble Mountain to the little town of **Takaka**, just inland from Golden Bay. At this point the South Island used to be connected to the North, which explains why plants and animals are still in a process of adaptation – a phenomenon of outstanding interest to botanists and zoologists. Near Takaka, watch the tame eels in the Anatoki River churn up the water as they're fed by hand. **Waikoropupu Springs**, close by, usually affectionately shortened to 'Pupu', are among the largest in the world, with a daily output of more than 2,000 million litres.

Bird-watchers will delight in **Farewell Spit**, a sanctuary for many species of birds, including two Arctic waders, the eastern bar-tailed godwit and the eastern knot, which migrate here annually from Siberia. Before they leave again, the male godwit's plumage changes to a regal red in preparation for courtship. March and April are the months to witness them depart in successive waves for far-distant breeding grounds in the northern tundra. Safaris take you up the Spit to the lighthouse. Golden Bay's most outlandish creature, however, is an outsize carnivorous snail. Do your snail-watching at **Kaihoka Lakes Scenic Reserve**.

The West Coast

West of the Alps, folk tales proliferate. Gold, coal, timber and greenstone form the background to stories of rivalry between Irish immigrants, improbable shanty- **67** towns, strong-willed women and hard-hitting, soft-spoken men – and of the West Coast's total refusal to kowtow to New Zealand drinking laws. In the days when pubs were required to close their doors at 6pm, the West Coasters simply smiled and kept on drinking. Many a local policeman quieted his conscience by knocking a firm admonition at the front door of a hotel before dodging round the back to down a friendly noggin. The first Europeans in these parts were sealers, then the 1860s saw the discovery of gold. Isolated, not very numerous, irrepressible and individualistic, the West Coasters add a touch of humour to the South Island scene.

The impressive scenery enlivens the drive from Inangahua Junction to Westport, through the Lower Buller Gorge. In 1929 the region was violently shaken by the Murchison earthquake. **Westport** (population 5,000) has a coal-mining past, well illustrated at the local mining museum. You can visit many of the **coal towns** including the ghost settlement of Denniston, Granity, where enormous oval boulders and a scatter-

That elusive nugget – or perhaps a few golden grains.

ing of gemstones litter the beach, and Stockton, site of an operational opencast mine. Punakaiki boasts 'pancake rocks' (limestone formations like giant flapjacks) and surf blowholes.

Mining was the *raison d'être* of **Greymouth**, locally known as 'Grey', the largest coastal town with a population of 8,500. Get into the spirit of the thing by taking a ride on the train that carried the miners through spectacular country to Rewanui Station. At the end of the line you can choose between a mine tour and a bush walk. **Shantytown** is a replica of a gold town – complete with a convincing-looking gaol and gallows. This is the place to try your hand at a little gold-panning.

Hokitika (population 3,600) still remembers when it was 'capital of the gold-fields'. Nowadays it's the capital of greenstone. You can visit the greenstone factories here and watch as craftsmen cut and polish this tough, attractive stone. The West Coast Historical Museum, noted for mining memorabilia, and Glow-worm Dell, 1½ kilometres north of the town, are also worth a visit. Lighting-up time is, of course, after dark.

Okarito Lagoon (turn off at The Forks before the Franz Josef Glacier) is marked by a tiny holiday settlement. Here, if you're lucky, you may glimpse the white heron *(Egretta alba)*, celebrated in Maori legend for its snowy plumage and graceful flight. The bird is rare in New Zealand. You'll need permission to visit the breeding grounds, north of Okarito. The main road continues south to Westland National Park.

Westland National Park
Two glaciers in this park, Franz Josef and Fox, rank among the scenic glories of New Zealand. Opinions vary as to which is the more impressive, but the question loses consequence when you stand confronted by the glittering majesty of these massive white-and-turquoise ice rivers thrusting into subtropical bushland. Both flow down from the snow-fields of the Alps to within a surprisingly short distance of the sea.

For full particulars of the excursions in the two areas, contact the Visitors' Centre at each place. The weather can change abruptly, so dress accordingly. Wear appropriate footgear and don't go for solitary strolls on the ice. Always inform someone of your intention if you decide to go on a lengthy hike. Guides are available and 69 necessary. All equipment, including boots and socks, is provided on guided trips. When the weather permits, there are scenic ski-plane and helicopter flights.

The **Franz Josef Glacier** was first sighted by Captain Cook as he sailed along the coast in 1769, but it was the geologist Julius von Haast who named it in 1862 after the emperor of his native Austria. Today's Franz Josef is a mere 7,000 years old, but it had an even grander parent – which reached right to the coast.

The glacier descends some 2,280 metres, terminating in a spectacular **icefall** that feeds the Waiho River (the name, 'Smoking Water', was inspired by the vapour rising from its surface). The river actually begins under the ice. The steepness of the glac-

Glaciers coexist side by side with subtropical bush in Westland.

ier's descent accounts for its low-altitude survival and the speed at which it moves: 5 metres a day has been recorded, but its average speed varies from a few centimetres to 1½ metres. Sometimes it even retreats, but at present it's advancing at 1 metre a day and terminates just 2 kilometres from the point noted by von Haast.

There are excellent walks in the area. Stop by **Peter's Pool**, a kettle-hole formed two centuries ago by a melted ice deposit left behind during the glacial retreat. **Sentinel Rock** is the biggest of a string of *roches moutonnées* (rocks which ice has sculpted into the shape of sheep). Note the extraordinarily rich growth of moss on the approach track. Roberts Point Track requires more effort. At **Lake Wombat** (another of the kettle-holes, an hour's walk from the road) you may see the rare great crested grebe. Some distance on, at **Christmas Lookout**, a meadow of snow grass is starred with alpine flowers.

For a unique view, visit **St James Anglican Church** (1931) where the chancel window reveals a scene of awe-inspiring mountain grandeur, forming a sublime backdrop to the altar.

Fox Glacier – named after a former New Zealand prime minister – plunges 14 kilometres to about 200 metres above sea level. For spectacular **views**, climb up to Cone Rock and Chalet Lookout. Mirror-like **Lake Matheson** catches chocolate-box reflections of snowy peaks and bush-covered hills. One of the best walks skirts the lake and takes an hour. The foliage is of exquisite beauty; so is the lake, which is usually unruffled. You'll be welcomed by

the sound of chiming bellbirds and accompanied by fantails. The walk to **Lake Gault** offers even more varied bird life. Very early morning is the best time for a visit. As for the glaciers themselves, try to be present at sunset, when the high peaks glow like opals, while the lower reaches withdraw into violet shadow. At Fox Glacier, you can visit the glow-worms for a last glimmer of magic before you turn in.

Christchurch

Often said to be 'the most English city outside England', Christchurch was intended as a home from home for settlers of Anglican persuasion. It has beautiful gardens and calm, orderly ways.

In 1850 the first settlers disembarked in Lyttelton Harbour. The Canterbury Pilgrims had been specially selected by home-town ministers, who were urged to ensure that they were sober, industrious, honest – and under 40. Inland, on a plain in the Canterbury district, they found their town ready planned and endowed with nostalgic street names.

Christchurch rapidly became the centre of a prosperous farming region. By the mid-1860s a million sheep grazed in Canter-

bury pastures. Today Canterbury lamb is world-famous, and the area rates as the country's chief grain producer.

At the heart of the city stands **Christchurch Cathedral**, built in early English Gothic style out of local stone. Pleasant buildings edge **Cathedral Square**. Marble tablets near the Post Office are inscribed with the names of the Canterbury Pilgrims.

Victoria Square sports a staid statue of the old queen and another of Captain Cook. The Town Hall, opened in 1972, overlooks the Avon River, named after a river in Scotland, so they say.

At the corner of Armagh and Durham streets, the **Provincial Council Buildings** are a splendid example of the revived Gothic style. Take a look at the Council Chamber (1865), decorated with the likenesses of Queen Victoria, Florence Nightingale, David Livingstone and the sculptor himself, William Brassington. The architect, Benjamin Mountfort, designed many of the city's most impressive buildings.

If you walk along Gloucester Street and then down Rolleston

A fountain shows its colours in English-style Christchurch.

Avenue you'll come to **Canterbury Museum**, another Mountfort building (1870); the Hall of Antarctic Studies there illustrates Christchurch's association with Antarctic exploration. The adjacent **McDougall Art Gallery** displays two Rodin sculptures. Both buildings are set in the Botanical Gardens area of Hagley Park. At nearby Christ's College – run on the lines of a traditional British public school – the boys still wear straw boaters.

Christchurch Arts Centre, further down Rolleston Avenue in the former Canterbury University buildings, boasts galleries, a cinema, theatre, craft workshop and pottery centre. At the office in the Clock Tower, in Worcester Street, ask for the key to **Rutherford's Den**, a small basement room that's now a mini-museum. Here the nuclear physicist Ernest Rutherford pursued his studies before transferring to Cambridge University in England.

Other Christchurch attractions include the **Royal New Zealand Airforce Museum** and the stunning sound-and-light show at the **International Antarctic Centre**. To visit some of the city's remarkable **private gardens**, inquire at the Tourist Office.

South of the city rise the Port Hills. Both the **Mt Cavendish Gondola** and the **Summit Road Drive**, along the crest of the hills, afford splendid views of the Canterbury Plains, with the Southern Alps to the west and Lyttelton Harbour to the east. Four roadhouses stand along the route, the most interesting of which, the Sign of the Takahe, resembles a Tudor hall, complete with carvings, coats of arms and heraldic shields. It now houses a tea-room.

You can go by foot along the **Bridle Path** from Christchurch to **Lyttelton**, following the Canterbury Pilgrims' journey in reverse.

For a scenic ride to remember, take the **Tranz-Alpine Express** through the Alps to Greymouth, or the **Coastal Pacific** along the Kaikoura coast to Picton.

Akaroa

French colonists settled Akaroa, 82 kilometres from Christchurch on the southern side of Banks Peninsula. This tiny place may seem more like a British seaside town than a French village, but souvenirs of its Gallic origins are cherished: the willows are said to have grown from cuttings transported from Napoleon's grave, old vineyards survive in places, and ancient fruit trees fill the air with scents as sweet as any found in a Normandy orchard. Family names and street names still reflect the town's beginnings as a supply station for French whalers – you can stroll along Rue Viard, Rue Lavaud and Rue Croix. On the foreshore a stone marks the place where the French landed. Nearby are trypots, vessels used for rendering whale blubber, and the Customs House. Exhibits at the **Langlois-Eteveneaux House and Museum** provide evocative glimpses of the early days.

Mt Cook National Park

Mt Cook stands at the centre of one of the country's finest parks, a world of cloud and ice, glacier and rock, mountain streams and alpine flowers. A giant among giants, New Zealand's highest mountain rises to a spectacular 3,764 metres. Surrounding it are scores of peaks with altitudes of 3,000 metres or more. Captain Cook never saw the mountain that is named after him, nor did Abel Tasman ever set eyes on Mt Tasman which, at 3,498 metres, is second only to Mt Cook.

The monarch of the Southern Alps, Aorangi ('Cloud-Piercer') to the Maoris, was first scaled on Christmas Day, 1894. Sir Edmund Hillary, conqueror of Mt Everest, numbers among many mountaineers who have tested themselves in the area. Only in 1970 was Mt Cook's most difficult face, the Caroline, climbed.

More than anything, it was glacial ice that sculpted the contours of the Southern Alps. The most famous of all the glaciers (among the longest in the world outside the polar regions) is the Tasman, 28 kilometres in length and up to 3 kilometres wide. One of the Tasman's subsidiaries, the Hochstetter, ends in a 1,000 metre descent so tortuous and chaotic that it is known as an icefall.

It was here that skiing in New Zealand had its beginnings, when three men shod themselves with elements of farm machinery to cross the area known as the Grand Plateau. The year was 1893. Foreign-made skis were introduced in 1909, but it was only after World War I that skiing grew in popularity. Today you can fly to the head of the **Tasman Glacier** for the ski experience of a lifetime, gliding 13 kilometres down the snow-covered ice river (experienced skiers only).

With **Mt Cook Village** and the most famous hotel in New

A river of ice and snow, Tasman Glacier is the skier's dream.

Zealand, the Hermitage, in the vicinity, this alpine area offers activities all the year round. Walking tops the list. Head out along Bowen Track to **Hooker Valley**, a good place to view Mt Cook. Or try the route to **Kea Point**, which passes through sub-alpine scrub and across moraine to a point overlooking Mueller Glacier, with the dizzy grandeur of Mt Sefton above. In summer you can branch off from the Kea Point walk to climb **Sealy Tarns**, abloom with native wild flowers. Another walk leads past the site of the first Hermitage Hotel (destroyed by a flood back in 1913), mounting eventually to **Copland Pass** (2,133 metres). Only experienced climbers accompanied by guides should attempt this latter route across the Main Divide to Fox Glacier on the West Coast.

Even in the harsh climate of Mt Cook, the wildlife flourishes. Tahr, chamois, red deer and hare were all introduced into the area, and now unfortunately damage the environment. Hunting is encouraged (you can obtain a permit from Park Headquarters).

Among birds, you'll see the rock wren, the grey warbler, the tiny rifleman and the plump native pigeon. You'll hear moreporks (the native owl) calling at night and will be amused and annoyed by the kea *(Nestor notabilis)*, a mountain parrot that seems a uniform drab green until it reveals brilliant scarlet under its wings. Keas are the biggest ragamuffins you're ever likely to meet. They steal food, toboggan down roofs, hang around campsites, hold up traffic for a mouthful of sandwich and gleefully rip to pieces anything you leave around, all the time keeping a wise and impudent eye on you.

The subtle beauty of the alpine flowers will enchant you. One of the most beguiling, the mountain buttercup or Mount Cook lily, blooms from November to January. There's also a busy insect life. The Visitor Centre distributes excellent brochures on the region's flora and fauna, which are of interest to both amateurs and specialists. The centre also advises on activities in the area.

A ride in a **ski-plane** (which has skis and retractable wheels) is an utterly unforgettable experience. You have a choice of itineraries. The most popular route, featuring the Fox and Franz Josef glaciers, includes a landing on one of the snow-fields.

Queenstown

Queenstown (population 3,300) lies in a bay on the shores of Lake Wakatipu, in sight of the beautiful Remarkables range. One of the most visited spots in the South Island, it offers all the attractions of lake and mountain (there's top-class skiing nearby at Coronet Peak), plus a roistering history of old gold days.

Local landmarks include the town's stone library (1877) and St Peter's Anglican Church. The Skyline Gondola wafts up Bob's Peak (446 metres) for a view of the town. Queenstown Motor Museum has a stirring display for veteran and vintage car enthusiasts (Brecon Street, at the foot of the gondola). The old cemetery nearby is full of memories: in particular, notice the plaques honouring the Chinese who flocked to the area in the 19th century, risking all to mine for gold. You can relive those heady days at the Sound and Light Museum. Or wander down the main street, a pedestrian-only mall, to Queenstown Gardens, on a small peninsula jutting out into the lake. The enormous boulder here commemorates explorer Captain Robert Falcon Scott of Antarctic fame.

Active romantics leave Queenstown at midnight to climb **Ben Lomond** (1,764 metres), so that they'll be sure to reach the summit in time to watch the sun rise over the Remarkables. Allow a full day to ascend the Remarkables themselves (2,342 metres).

Down on **Lake Wakatipu** you'll meet a grand old lady, the *Earnslaw*, a coal-burning steamer built in Dunedin in 1912, the last of several to ply the waters. The

Earnslaw may be getting on, but she has young ideas: lunchtime champagne cruises, poetry read-

---

The Demon Lake

The name Wakatipu ('Where the Demon Lies') has its origins in a myth which recounts that a love-struck giant once abducted a Maori princess and brought her to this spot. Worn out by the emotional strain and a particularly irritating nor'westerly wind, he lay down to sleep .Then up crept the girl's lover who set fire to the giant's bed of dry fern. As the demon died he burned deep into the earth until all that was left was a great S-shaped hollow, which soon filled up with rain and melting snow. At the bottom of the lake his heart still beats, which accounts for the strange pulsation of the lake waters.

Tilling the soil – farmers at work in agricultural Lumsden.

ings, believe-it-or-not gold-rush yarns and evening dine-and-dance dos. You may prefer to take a less colourful but faster launch to one of the big **sheep stations**, Cecil Peak or Walter Peak. They lay on a sheep-dog display, a general meet-the-animals session, an exhibition of woolcraft, and a huge afternoon tea for tourists.

You can fish the lake for rainbow and brown trout and quinnat salmon, but there's also **bungy jumping** and there are **jet-boat trips** where you move so fast that the scenery blurs. Try the Kawarau or the Shotover River experience and you'll be talking about it for the rest of your life. Not quite so nerve-tingling, though almost, are the **raft trips** on the river.

At **Deer Park Heights** the tahr, wapiti, chamois and mountain goats live in a natural setting. From here there's a fine view of mountains, rivers and lakes.

The **Golden Terrace Mining Village**, about 3 kilometres from Queenstown, recreates the atmosphere of the roaring '60s. A real goldrush town exists 21 kilometres away: the deserted mining centre of **Arrowtown**, enchanting in summer, a dream of smoky amber and bright gold in autumn, as the old trees change colour for the winter and the air is crisp with early frost. Wood and stone cottages, the homes of miners long gone, border the main street.

Near Arrowtown are **Gibbstown Vineyard** and the luxurious resort of **Millbrook**, which has a magnificent golf course.

If you didn't miss a heartbeat jet-boating, then test yourself on **Skippers Canyon**, where guided tours traverse a narrow, stony road edged by precipitous drops. Huge amounts of gold came out of Skippers. The wild roses that bloom all around were planted by the miners to provide rosehip syrup to supplement their scanty

Jet-boating – thrills of a lifetime, just sit back and scream.

diet. While your driver is brewing tea in the cabin at the end of the road, take a pan to the river and try your luck. The odd grain or two may still be found.

Two of New Zealand's best guided hikes start from Queenstown: both the **Routeburn** and the **Hollyford Valley Walk** wind through bush and alpine landscape. If you drive from Queenstown to Te Anau, you'll pass the town of **Kingston**. In summer a restored 1915 steam locomotive, the *Kingston Flyer*, proudly puffs its way from here to Fairlight.

Fiordland

New Zealand's biggest national park is a hauntingly beautiful world of wild valleys, soaring mountains and startlingly blue water. Parts of Fiordland are still unexplored, and the area remains sparsely populated. The big fur-seal colonies here attracted some of the earliest European settlers.

Te Anau

Visitors know Te Anau as a halting place from which to explore the glorious wilderness of New Zealand's south-west corner. Set on the shore of the South Island's biggest lake, it is the gateway to the Fiordland National Park. The 81 town lives from tourism and deer, culling breeding stock from the hundreds of introduced animals that multiply in the bush. The venison is exported for sale in the European market. Red deer seriously menace Fiordland ecology, destroying vegetation and causing erosion. Helicopters, nets and tranquillizer guns are used to fly them out of inaccessible places.

Up in the Murchison Range, above the township, live the last of the takahe *(Notornis mantelli)* – flightless birds with brilliant indigo and viridian plumage and a rounded reddish bill. Believed extinct, they were rediscovered in 1948. Thanks to careful conservation, several hundred pairs now thrive in a part of the forest kept strictly out of bounds.

The very day the takahe was found, a new cave was discovered in the area, **Te Anau-au** ('Cave of Whirling Water'). The only 'living' cave in New Zealand, it is still being formed by water rushing in from Lake Orbell. The cave lies across the lake from the town. A quiet night-time launch trip makes the perfect introduction. You journey within the cave to an underground waterfall, then to a chamber lit by huge glow-worms. The country's second deepest lake, secretively beautiful **Manapouri** (a corruption of Manawapouri, 'Lake of the Sorrowing Heart'), was saved thanks to public protest when schemes were afoot to raise its level to generate hydro-electricity. A day trip takes you to the lake and out into **Doubtful Sound**. You can also visit the West Arm Underground Powerhouse, the country's largest power station. A tunnel of roughhewn rock leads down to the plant, 213 metres below ground.

There are scenic flights from Te Anau and many trails in the area. **Milford Track**, the 'finest walk in the world', starts at the head of Lake Te Anau. Hire packs and waterproofs at the Te Anau hotel. Pre-booking is essential.

Visitors to Fiordland National Park should make a point of dropping in at Park Headquarters, on Te Anau Terrace, for information and useful publications.

The Road to Milford

You can walk, drive or fly to Milford Sound. Each method offers its own delights. The road passes through patchy tussock, snowgrass and stretches of gravel into the superb beech forest of **Eglinton Valley**. You'll feel as though you're entering a lost world – and so, in a way, you are, for the 1,500,000 hectares of this park have a lonely splendour, which you sense and see as the silence closes in and mountains crowd above the dark, dripping forest.

Pause at the **Mirror Lakes**, to admire the flawless reflections, then follow the Avenue of the Disappearing Mountain – a peak seems to get smaller as you approach, then, suddenly reappears, its snowcapped tip sparkling, its lower slopes daubed with bright mosses and lichens.

On the other side of Knobs Flat, a track leads to Lake Gunn.

Further along you come to Lakes Fergus and Lochie. Linger by **Falls Creek**, just on from the Hollyford Valley turnoff, in order to admire the tumbling cascade. The road then climbs steeply up to **Homer Tunnel**. Here a well-organized gang of mountain parrots habitually mounts a hold-up in the hope of extorting a tasty handout. **The Chasm** offers a good view of the Cleddau River, writhing its way through worn rocks. From here, eleven slow, winding and infinitely rewarding kilometres complete the journey to sea level and Milford Sound.

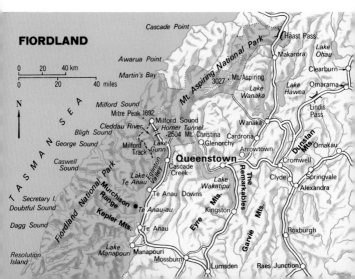

Milford Sound

More rain falls on Milford Sound in a year than just about anywhere else in the country – over 6,000 millimetres. But rain does not detract from the splendour of the place, for it glistens on the trees, lends an ethereal glow to the mosses, and sets a thousand waterfalls leaping. On a good day the surface of the Sound is as smooth as polished greenstone.

Since it was created by glacial action, Milford Sound is actually a fiord, one of many in the area. No commercial fishing is carried out here, although the salt water contains barracuda, cod and tuna, and thousands of tiny mussels gleam on the rocks at the water's edge. The fishing boats you see moored in the Sound set off to the coast, where the crayfish are huge and succulent and numerous.

Whatever else you do at Milford Sound, take one of the **launch trips** on offer. Clasping your insect repellent firmly in one hand and waving the other vigorously across your face (this is vicious sandfly country), walk or take a shuttle bus to the wharf near Bowen Falls.

Elemental majesty – the lonely
84 *fastnesses of Fiordland.*

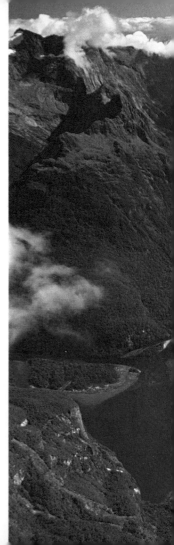

From your boat you'll see the misty 150-metre drop of **Stirling Falls**, sheer mountains where the trees grow so closely matted in the thin soil that they actually provoke 'bush avalanches'. You will also see baby seals locking their flippers together in order to float on the surface or sunbathing on warm grandstand rocks, while dolphins perform a special turn around the boat.

Of all the places you visit in New Zealand, this isolated, ice-carved paradise may well be the memory that lasts the longest. As you go along, a sensitive commentary from the knowledgeable

crew provides you with interesting information about the Sound without disturbing your mood.

Dunedin

Warm-hearted, canny, far-sighted Dunedin richly deserves its title 'the Edinburgh of the South'. You will be aware of a subtle speech difference – the distinctive roll of the Scottish 'r', which persists after generations of settlement.

Dunedin (population 110,000) made its money as a banking centre in gold rush days and has been quietly defending and increasing it ever since. First in education, Dunedin acknowledges its status as a university town by taking a parental pride in the successes of its students – and displaying a mature tolerance of their pranks. The emphasis is on medical studies at New Zealand's oldest university (and for 100 years the only medical college).

Start your tour at the **Octagon**, in the centre of town, a square embellished with a statue of the Scots poet Robert Burns. He's portrayed sitting with 'his back to the kirk and his face to the pub'. In fact, the kirk (St Paul's Anglican Cathedral) has outlived the pub, which has been demolished. Burns also chooses to turn his back on the Municipal Chambers (1880) and currently faces the Star Musical Fountain.

Stuart Street is the site of the dignified Law Courts, which provide a dour, sober contrast to the

You can count sheep day or night – right up to 70 million!   **87**

marvellously exuberant Railway Station further along. The **Early Settlers' Museum** nearby has a collection of pioneer and gold-rush mementoes. Opinion is divided as to the merits of the Cargill Monument (High Street), commemorating Captain William Cargill, who was one of the co-founders of the Free Church of Scotland settlement in Otago.

On the southern side of Moray Place a soaring spire draws the eye to First Church (1868–73), an example of the Neo-Gothic style. Knox Church, in George Street, leading from the Octagon, is the work of the same architect, R. A. Lawson.

The **Otago Museum** (Great King Street) houses an outstanding collection of Maori, Melanesian and other Pacific Island material, including an ornately carved meeting-house. There are also extensive ceramic displays, notably of Greek and Roman origin, plus natural history exhibits and a special section devoted to the history of shipping.

The **Dunedin Public Art Gallery** includes paintings by those 18th-century rivals Joshua Reynolds and Thomas Gainsborough. There are also fine works by the internationally acclaimed painter Frances Hodgkins, who was born in Dunedin.

Built of stone and roofed in slate, the imposing **Otago University Buildings** (Castle Street) reflect the importance the city has always placed on education.

Don't miss **Olveston House**, a gracious Edwardian residence richly decorated with European furniture and objects, bequeathed to the city by the last surviving member of the cultured and much-travelled Theomin family.

Another admirable building is **Larnach's Castle**, erected in 1871. Decorating the interior of this baronial hall are remarkable carvings by a British artist who spent 12 years at the task.

Bird-lovers will want to visit **Taiaroa Head** at the tip of Otago Peninsula, one of the few places in the world where you can see a colony of one of the world's largest birds – the northern royal albatross. Access is strictly controlled; contact the Visitor Information Centre, 48 The Octagon, Dunedin, to obtain information about visiting the site.

The Far South

Like Dunedin, **Invercargill** (with an urban population of 54,000) has a Scottish background. Well-

planned and conservative, New Zealand's most southerly city claims no great tourist attractions, nor does it need them; for this is one of the most prosperous areas in the country, drawing its wealth from agriculture and food processing. You'll see big freezing plants all round the town.

Bluff, 27 kilometres to the south, is no beauty spot. But it is a busy trading and fishing port,

Join the team or go it alone – there's a sport for everyone.

known throughout the country for its oysters. From here boats depart for **Stewart Island**, some 30 kilometres away across the Foveaux Strait.

Few New Zealanders have visited Stewart Island and fewer than 400 live there – most of them in **Oban**, the island's main and only town. Oban stands at the head of Halfmoon Bay, where a museum of Stewart Island history and natural history usually opens on the day when the Bluff boat comes in. There are almost no roads and little commerce, a few farmers, a storekeeper or two and a number of fishermen. You can explore the northern area – but the south is almost untouched, so don't go far without adequate advice.

If you can, visit **Ulva Island** in Paterson Inlet, a nature reserve with sandy beaches and a marvellous variety of ferns and orchids. Stewart Islanders will tell you that the bushparrots here get so drunk from sipping nectar that they can often hardly make it to the next tree. It may well be true, for Stewart Island is the last and loneliest spot of all.

A gourmet's delight – succulent bluff crayfish, ocean fresh.

What to Do

Sports

In New Zealand, physical fitness is a way of life. Everybody plays tennis, football or hockey, skates or skis, jumps, jogs, hurls a discus, dives or does gymnastics. And people are more than just fit, they're tough. Don't try to emulate them. If you're undertaking one of the country's celebrated walks or raft trips, remember that exposure can be dangerous. New Zealanders may get away with facing untamed nature in shorts and boots – but you may not.

Getting Involved

Golf is played year-round in New Zealand, which boasts more than 300 registered golf clubs. Private clubs accord guest courtesies to members of clubs overseas; bring along a letter of introduction from your home-club secretary. Every town has public courses.

New Zealanders are practically born with a tennis racket in their hand. The season runs from October to May. Every district has a club, and you'll be given a warm welcome at any of them.

A sizeable number of retired New Zealanders take up bowls, played outdoors on meticulously maintained lawns. Tradition decrees appropriate apparel: white flannels and panama hat for men, over-the-knee sports dress and hat for women.

Water Sports

There's not much you can do in water that you can't do in New Zealand. Always within easy reach of the sea and with innumerable lakes and rivers at hand, New Zealanders enjoy water sports enormously. Swimming, surfing and sailing count among the most popular. The sea, however, seldom gets really warm.

When swimming, take the usual precaution of staying near people. Heed warnings on dangerous beaches. Drowning accidents are tragically frequent, but common sense should keep you out of trouble. Take adequate precautions lest a sunburn spoil your holiday.

Get under sail in the boating season, from November to May. A number of companies charter fully-equipped yachts, with or without crew. Address enquiries to the New Zealand Tourist and Publicity Office or New Zealand Yacht Charter Association, Post Office, Opua, Bay of Islands.

Fishing

There's plenty of game fish for the taking in New Zealand's off-shore waters. Go after black and striped marlin, broadbill or mako, thresher, hammer-head and blue shark, yellowtail and five species of tuna during the deep-sea fishing season (mid-January through April). Bases are at Whangaroa, Bay of Islands, Whangarei (Tutukaka), Mercury Bay (Whitianga), Tauranga (Mayor Island) and Whakatane (Whale Island and White Island).

You don't need a licence, but you must abide by the limit of four fish per day from the sword family. The modern, highspeed launches available for charter can accommodate from one to six people; many have flying bridges. The captain provides tackle. If you use your own (excellent tackle is on sale in New Zealand), remember that it needs to comply with International Game Fishing Association rules. Note that the swordfish species can only be taken by rod and line.

Join a local deep-sea fishing club. Membership is inexpensive, and they'll provide weighing equipment and issue certificates, invaluable for convincing those scoffers back home.

Both rainbow and brown trout were released into New Zealand waters during the last century. Now there are thousands of them. Even if you've never held a fishing rod in your hands before, have a go at angling while you're here. Dozens of novices bring in whoppers every year.

If you're a dedicated angler, you'll make plenty of friends, swap endless yarns and be taken to little-known pools where huge fish disport in limpid water. A special monthly Tourist Fishing Licence is available, in addition to weekly and day licences.

Some areas are set aside for fly-fishing. If not specified, they are open to trolling, threadlining and bait-casting. Fly-fishing rods need to be less flexible than in many countries, in order to cast into the wind and handle heavy fish. Imported or locally made tackle can be bought or hired throughout the country. It's best to select flies in New Zealand. If possible, bring your own chest or thigh-waders with you – they are not always available for hire.

Limits vary, but you can count on six to ten rainbow trout per

Taut canvas, curling breakers … the sea offers boundless fun.

angler per day, and any number of brown trout. Size limits vary, too. Generally, anything under 35 centimetres must be returned.

Experienced guides with cars and launches are available in the main angling areas. Helicopters can take you to out-of-the-way fishing spots. And there's even a guided fishing tour of New Zealand, taking in both islands.

River-Rafting

If you're fit – and aren't too faint-hearted – consider river-rafting in an inflatable rubber boat. You can indulge in a few hours of thrills or, if you're an enthusiast,

spend several days rafting, camping onshore as you go. The high excitement of negotiating rapids, manoeuvring bends and plunging down waterfalls alternates with passages of placid paddling.

Trout for the taking, and plenty of challenging mountains to climb.

Organized rafting tours are accompanied by guides graded by the New Zealand Professional Rafting Association. Not only are they knowledgeable about various regions, but they also do the cooking and can administer first-aid. Life jackets and crash helmets are provided.

To participate, you must be of a certain age and able to swim. Depending on the weather, you should wear a wetsuit or woollen clothing (jeans and cotton cloth-ing aren't recommended). Rivers are graded according to difficul-ty. Some tours combine rafting with other activities – hiking, fishing, even panning for gold.

Hiking

New Zealand has thousands of kilometres of tracks suitable for hiking. The 53-kilometre Milford Track on the South Island is the best known, but there's a big choice throughout the country, including the Routeburn (40km), the Hollyford (27km) and the Abel Tasman Coastal Trek. Many of the routes traverse the superb national parks.

As you hike, you'll see New Zealand's landscape at its finest – the clear lakes and tumbling waterfalls, grottoes of tree-ferns, unspoiled forest and native birds. People of all ages can manage the less arduous routes, but don't overestimate your endurance.

Hunting

Game animals can be stalked year round, without licence or limit. You can bag red, sika and fallow deer, chamois, tahr, wild goat, boar, rabbit, hare, opossum and wallaby. It's best to use a guide; they operate in the wild or on their own protected lands.

Gamebirds, waterfowl, pheasant and quail have a limited season, and licences are required.

Skiing

New Zealand offers skiers plenty of powder snow and a season (July to October) that coincides with the northern hemisphere summer. Of the country's 20 or so recognized ski-fields, some belong to clubs and are reserved for use by club members only.

North Island's skiing centres include Mt Ruapehu, in Tongariro National Park, and Turoa, site of the highest vertical ski lift in Australasia (720m). On the South Island, Mt Hutt has an exceptionally long season, while

On the ball! The All Blacks very rarely lose a match.

Tekapo is sunny, with good powder snow. Tasman Glacier offers grandiose scenery and helicopter lifts to virgin snow for experienced skiers. Coronet Peak, close to Queenstown, ranks among the world's best skifields.

Spectator Sports

New Zealanders are dedicated horse-racing fans, and a number of world-famous thoroughbreds have been raised here. Trotting events and greyhound races often take place at night under floodlighting. Off-course bets can be placed at authorized TAB (Totalisator Agency Board) offices in all centres.

New Zealand's international rugby team, the All Blacks, is known all round the world. Here rugby is more than a game – it's a tradition, an art, almost a religion! Even five-year-olds practise drop kicks and punts at home and tear over the school sports fields at lunchtime and after class, dreaming of celebrity to come. Rugby (the most popular form of football) and soccer matches draw crowds from June through September. You'll need to reserve for the major matches. Cricket, played November through April, has a sizeable following, too.

Shopping

Shopping in New Zealand is a chatty business. Before you can make a purchase you'll probably be asked where you are from – and may even even be invited for a weekend's fishing!

Sheepskins are high on the list of specialities; there's a huge selection from single pelts to rugs. Sheepskins are made into car-seat covers, coats, boots and hats. You'll find natural white, brown and black, as well as a range of artificial colours. Natural fleece underblankets are excellent for invalids and babies since they allow the air to circulate. Stringent tests are applied to sheepskin products, and you can have confidence in a label that carries the 'machine-washable' mark.

Woollen goods make excellent buys, including hand-knitted sweaters and a fine assortment of blankets, travel and floor rugs. Spinning and weaving are a thriving cottage industry in New Zealand. Some woollen articles are coloured with vegetable dyes.

Local craftsmen fashion New Zealand timber into a variety of **wooden articles**, such as bowls, plates, goblets, trays, bookends and – for children – attractive chunky toys, puzzles, and inlaid rulers and pencil-boxes. You'll encounter smooth golden kauri, attractively grained reddish rimu, brown rata and dark hinau. Small items, especially vases, are also made out of *ponga* (fernwood).

Maori carving can reach a superb standard of painstaking traditional craftsmanship. Gourds incised with Maori motifs make attractive containers for dried flowers, or highly unusual wine and water decanters. Maori designs taken from rock drawings and carvings decorate tablemats, napkins, bath towels, ashtrays, earrings, T-shirts and carrier bags – you name it and some enthusiast somewhere has produced it.

Look for **jewellery** and **ornaments** made from semi-precious stones, shell, bone and wood. Greenstone, which is a kind of jade, ranges in colour from pale to dark green. You will find it carved into simple, tasteful pendants, bracelets, cufflinks, rings and paperknives and used in the handles of coffee spoons and fruit knives. Variations on the Maori fishhook look best worn suspended on a flax or leather thong. Bone is similarly worked. Paua, an iridescent shell shot with green and blue, is used to

The traditions of old are proudly preserved by today's artists.

enhance jewel, cigarette and card boxes. Distinctive pieces of jewellery may also incorporate paua – which is similar to abalone but more colourful. Rich, golden **99** kauri gum and petrified wood are mounted in pendants, earrings and the like. Opals are imported from Australia and can be purchased in jewellery and specialist shops throughout the country.

New Zealand has a thriving **leather** industry. 'Possum and deer skins are made into coats, bags and hats. Chamois is shaped into soft, elegant clothing. You need have no stirrings of ecological guilt. The deer multiply fast and have to be culled to protect the forests. They are also farmed.

Remember that **historic artefacts** such as clubs *(meres)*, fertility symbols *(tikis)*, whalebone ear pendants and old carvings cannot be taken out of the country without permission from the Ministry of Internal Affairs.

There's no shortage of **souvenir items.** Perfumes and toilet powders based on the essence of native New Zealand flowers make attractive gifts. Children warm to big cuddly kiwis with funny felt beaks, and a variety of Maori dolls dressed in traditional flax skirts and imitation kiwi cloaks. Recordings run the gamut from Maori chants and war-dances to the latest rock groups. Books cover every conceivable subject, including colonial architecture,

photographic studies, anthropological surveys and cooking. And don't forget New Zealand wines and liqueurs; the latter are often made from subtropical fruits or native shrubs. The honey, especially from flowering indigenous plants, is delicious – but pack with care or your globe-trotting may come to a sticky end. To carry home all your loot, why not buy a handwoven flax bag? They are available in a variety of sizes.

Entertainment

New Zealanders are just as keen on a night out as anybody else, but you can't expect a great concentration of sophisticated entertainment in a country that has a population of only 3½ million.

Larger towns have nightclubs and discos, and many hotels and restaurants feature good bands and name entertainers. Cinema flourishes (New Zealand is in the film-making business these days). New Zealand opera and ballet companies and the National Orchestra tour the country regularly. Many international artists (from classical to pop, folk and rock) appear in New Zealand.

You'll find plenty of community activity and tremendous en-

The Haka

Haka *means rhythmic dancing, but nowadays it refers to the war dance which the Maoris used to perform before battle. Stamping, rolling of eyes and poking out of tongues helped get the men into fighting spirit.*

The haka you are most likely to hear is attributed to a chief called Te Rauparaha. One of his friends, noted for his unusually hairy appearance, hid him in a food pit to keep him safe from his enemies. When Te Rauparaha re-emerged into the daylight, he expressed his appreciation in a resounding haka *that is performed to this day by national sports teams. Most New Zealanders know the words, so, when things get going, why not join in?*

Ka mate! Ka mate!	It is death! It is death!
Ka ora! Ka ora!	It is life! It is life!
Tenei te tangata puhuruhuru,	This is the hairy person
Nana nei i tiki mei	Who made the sun shine!
I whakawhiti re ra!	
Upane! Upane!	One step up! Another step up!
Upane! Kaupane!	One last step up! The step out!
Whiti te ra!	Into the sunlight!

thusiasm for the arts, both in rural localities and in towns. People go in for everything from madrigal singing to Highland dancing.

Don't miss the Maori concerts in Rotorua. The performers enjoy them as much as the audience. You'll see pretty girls performing tenderly graceful *poi* dances (the *poi* is a fibre ball twirled on a length of twine), stick games and action dances. The men demonstrate hand games devised to train warriors for alertness in battle, and will do their best to scare the wits out of you with a *haka*.

You'll hear some so-called Maori songs. Delightful as they are, the music is Europeanized. In early times the musical range was smaller and the main instrument was a type of flute. There were no drums. Rhythm was produced by clapping, stamping and slapping. The concerts are well commentated in several languages; they are very relaxed, and sooner or later everybody joins in.

Look out for the agricultural shows, which often feature some fine show-jumping, plus typical New Zealand competitions such as axe-chopping, sheep-shearing and sheepdog trials, involving a fascinating display of telepathy **102** between master and dog.

Eating Out

Until a few years ago, traditional British eating habits held sway. Then the pendulum swung the other way. Experimentation was rife. Now New Zealand is cultivating a mature approach to cuisine. Chefs from overseas have brought their *savoir faire* with them. Classic French cooking is greatly appreciated, but subtle and distinctive tastes are being incorporated and a recognizably national style is evolving. Often it bears resemblance to French *nouvelle cuisine*. After all, New Zealand is the world's major producer of kiwifruit – almost the hallmark of *nouvelle cuisine*.

Strict liquor laws and lack of wine-making traditions formed older generations into a beer-drinking nation. Then Yugoslav immigrants planted some of the country's first vineyards. New Zealanders are still slightly astonished that they are now successfully producing quantities of wine, that it's getting better all the time, and that their critical faculties are keeping pace.

Some restaurants possess full liquor licences, others are unlicensed. Certain establishments carry a BYO sign ('Bring your own'). You arrive with the wine you've bought yourself, and the waiter chills it if necessary and serves it in the normal way.

Most towns of any size boast a variety of exotic eating-places, (French, Italian, Chinese, Indian and Indonesian). International fast-food chains are well represented – as are vegetarian and health-food establishments. Living as they do in the lap of gastronomic plenty, New Zealanders try to be diet conscious.

Take-away stalls specializing in fresh fish and chips, deep-fried oysters and mussels or paua fritters can provide you with a regal repast. Lots of pubs serve simple meals (good value at lunchtime); coffee shops and wine bars also offer sandwiches and simple hot dishes. American-style hamburgers and milkshakes are popular. Or you can do your own buying at grocery shops and delicatessens, and enjoy a picnic lunch in one of the parks or squares.

Soups and Starters

New Zealand produces an almost embarrassing quantity of excellent foodstuffs – lamb, vegetables, fruit, dairy products. The superb fish and shellfish include varieties found nowhere else.

Keep an eye open for typical dishes incorporating the indigenous toheroa, a type of clam. These shellfish, which can grow to a considerable size, are dug with wooden spades from certain beaches during a restricted winter season. The toheroa can be baked in the shell, minced, coated in pastry and fried or, most often, made into a rich, strong soup. Look, too, for its close cousin, the smaller, sweeter tuatua.

Seafood pâtés, including crayfish and smoked eel, can be very good. Sample the popular 'raw' fish starter made from terakihi, a firm-fleshed sea fish that's marinated in lemon juice and served in imported coconut milk.

Seafood

New Zealand waters teem with fish and shellfish. The fishermen bring in excellent scallops, crayfish (spiny lobster) and oysters by the boatload, as well as flounder, sole and delicately flavoured John Dory. Restaurant menus feature snapper, the most plentiful variety, and groper *(hapuka)*, a popular deep-water species. Kingfish is prized but not widely available. Order the densely textured ling, baked or steamed. You'll also come across piper, **103** best fried, bonito, served in steaks, squid, and marlin that has been smoke-cured.

Freshwater rivers produce delicate little whitebait, delectably pan-fried in butter. You may eat sockeye and quinnat salmon in restaurants – but not brown or rainbow trout, since they are classified as game fish.

Don't hold back, help yourself! It's all there for the asking.

Meat and Game

Lamb comes out tops, tender and fragrantly seasoned. New Zealanders like it roasted and served with mint sauce or mint jelly, British style. Try crown of lamb with a tangy tamarillo sauce. Prepared well, this garnet-coloured subtropical fruit proves the perfect complement. Captain Cook released the first pigs into the bush. Old-timers still call them 'Captain Cookers'. Suckling pig

and wild boar are excellent. So is venison, often prepared in a wine sauce with mushrooms. Quail and pheasant are sometimes served with mountain berries.

Vegetables

All the familiar vegetables are grown in New Zealand – from leeks, lettuces and cauliflower to capsicum and avocados. Thanks to the benign climate, vegetables tend to grow larger and have a stronger flavour than in Europe, For a change of pace, try the native *kumara* (sweet potato) and *kumi-kumi* (a type of pumpkin). Fresh New Zealand asparagus may be the best in the world.

Cheese and Butter

New Zealand's celebrated dairy products include yoghurt and excellent cheeses. Among the latter, there's a choice of cheddar (mild or tangy), camembert, brie, blue vein, Greek-style *feta* (packed in brine) and port-wine and smoked cheese, as well as cheeses and spreads that are flavoured with herbs, chives or sesame. Eat New Zealand cheese with locally produced crispbreads, crackers and breads, including long French loaves and whole-grain products. All those contented-looking cows you see contribute to the quality of the butter: it owes its yellow colour to the carotene content of the grass, not to any additives.

Fruit

Although New Zealanders eat a lot of pineapple, it doesn't grow here, nor do papayas, mangoes, coconuts, avocados or bananas, all of which are imported. What you will see in quantity are passionfruit, kiwifruit, oranges and

105

tangelos – a delicious cross between a mandarin and a grapefruit bursting with juice. You will also come across feijoas, a small green semi-tropical fruit. Apples, pears, peaches, cherries, apricots and nectarines thrive in various regions. In season, the luscious strawberries, raspberries, cherries and blackberries are a must.

Desserts

Sample the ice-cream, especially the semi-tropical fruit flavours. Cakes and pastries layered with fresh whipped cream are a tempting trap for weight-watchers. The art reaches a dizzy peak in the national favourite, Pavlova cake, a mammoth meringue, slightly sticky on the inside, crisp on the outside, filled and topped with cream and decorated with fruit (even dedicated dieters will surrender). Runner-up for first place is cheesecake. British visitors will warm to home treats like treacle pudding, and hot apple pie well studded with cloves.

Drinks

Quench your thirst with the bottled beer, stout and cider. New Zealanders tend to go in for short drinks. As a mixer, try Lemon and Paeroa Water from a North Island mineral spring.

Imported wines are available but expensive, and locally produced vintages offer far better value for money. Both whites and reds – some of which are internationally renowned – are readily available and well worth investigating. New Zealand also produces sherry and port, as well as kiwifruit wines. Ti-Toki liqueur is distilled from native berries and shrubs.

You'll find that, by European standards, the coffee is weak, the tea good and strong.

The Hangi

Every visitor to New Zealand should sample a Maori feast, a scrumptious spread of meats and seafood prepared in an earth oven (hangi). The word hangi *also applies to any social gathering where hangi-cooked food is eaten. A big pit is dug in the ground and heated stones are placed at the bottom. The food, enclosed in flax bags, is lowered in, covered with leaves, wet cloths and a layer of earth, and allowed to steam. Although the accent is on Maori favourites such as smoked eel, fish, mussels and a small shellfish known as the pipi, European tastes are admitted, too. You'll find tender suckling pig, chicken, lamb and venison. European desserts usually round off the feast.*

BLUEPRINT for a Perfect Trip

How to Get There

Because of the complexity and variability of the many fares, you should ask the advice of an informed travel agent well before your departure.

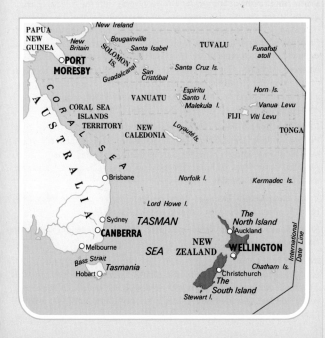

BY AIR

From Australia: Regular direct flights link Sydney and Auckland several times daily. In addition, carriers offer direct flights from Adelaide, Cairns, Brisbane, Darwin, Melbourne, Perth and Townsville to Auckland, as well as from Brisbane, Melbourne, Sydney and Perth to Christchurch, and Brisbane, Melbourne and Sydney to Wellington. Main types of fares: first-class, business, economy, special fares.

From Japan: Scheduled flights leave Tokyo for Auckland and Christchurch direct several times a week. One-stop connections are available through Bangkok, Singapore, Bali and Hong Kong. Main types of fares: first-class, business, economy, special fares.

From North America: Auckland is connected with the following cities several times a week: Honolulu (mostly non-stop flights), Los Angeles (non-stop or 1 or 2 stops), New York (2 stops), San Francisco (1 stop). From other cities in the US, or from Canada, you'll have to change aircraft in New York, Los Angeles or Honolulu. Main types of fares: first-class, business, economy, Point-to-Point. For such a distance, it may be worth considering the round-the-world deals offered by several airlines; they allow the passenger to stop en route (Honolulu, Tahiti, Fiji, South-East Asia, for example).

From the British Isles: There are several regular weekly flights from London to New Zealand with 1, 2 or 3 stops en route. Otherwise, you'll need to change aircraft in either Singapore, Hong Kong, Sydney or Los Angeles. Main types of fares: first-class, business, economy, Excursion, YOX (one-way Excursion).

From Continental Europe: New Zealand can be reached from most major European cities, with 1 stop in a major Asian city.

From South America: There is a direct weekly flight linking Auckland and Buenos Aires.

Package tours

A wide choice of package tours is available: fly/drive arrangements (with or without accommodation), camper or motorhome rentals, fully escorted coach holidays, escorted budget coach holidays, farm holidays, trekking holidays, ski packages.

Domestic flights

Air New Zealand is the primary domestic carrier, with Ansett New Zealand in competition on main trunk routes. Mount Cook Airlines operates mainly from cities to resort areas, and a number of smaller companies serve provincial towns. There are frequent flights from main centres, provincial towns and resort areas.

Discount tickets

Before departure, overseas tourists can buy an Air New Zealand Pass, valid for specific periods of travel on domestic airlines. The Kiwi-Coach Pass allows unlimited travel with the larger motor coach companies and reductions on certain excursions. You can buy this pass before departure, or on arrival if onward international travel documents are presented. New Zealand Railways' Travelpass is valid for travel by train, coach and ferry. It entitles holders to some accommodation and other travel discounts, too.

When to Go

The climate is subtropical in the North Island and temperate in the South Island. When planning your trip, remember that the seasons are topsy turvy for people from the northern hemisphere: summer is from December through February; autumn from March through May; winter from June through August; spring from September through November. Although December decorations pay tribute to Yuletide snow and holly, Christmas comes in summer and you're quite likely to spend it at the beach, where the pohutukawa, New Zealand's own 'Christmas tree', will be in full scarlet flower along the cliffs. Labour Day (fourth Monday in October) heralds the warmer weather. Main school holidays run from mid-December to early February, so make reservations well in advance for this peak period.

Average daily maximum temperatures

		J	F	M	A	M	J	J	A	S	O	N	D
Auckland	°F	74	75	74	68	63	59	58	59	63	64	68	71
	°C	23	24	23	20	17	15	14	15	17	18	20	22
Christchurch	°F	71	71	67	63	57	52	52	54	59	63	67	69
	°C	22	22	19	17	14	11	11	12	15	17	19	21

Planning Your Budget

To give you an idea of what to expect, here's a list of average prices in New Zealand dollars (NZ$). The prices below include the 12.5% Goods and Service Tax (GST). Always check if the GST has been included in the marked price.

Airport departure tax. NZ$ 20.

Airport transfers. *Wellington:* Bus from airport to city centre NZ$ 4, 'super shuttle' NZ$ 8–38, taxi NZ$ 15. *Auckland:* Bus NZ$ 10, 'super shuttle' NZ$ 14–23, taxi NZ$ 35. *Christchurch:* Bus NZ$ 2.40, 'super shuttle' NZ$ 8–20, taxi NZ$ 18.

Buses. City buses: NZ$ 1.20 per zone. Coach: Wellington–Auckland NZ$ 96, budget NZ$ 67; Chrsitchurch–Dunedin NZ$ 51, budget $37.

Camping. Motor camps NZ$ 15, camping sites NZ$ 6–8 per person.

Car hire (international company). *Mitsubishi Lancer* (or similar 4-seater) NZ$ 144 per day for 1–2 days, NZ$ 103 per day for 3–13 days, NZ$ 100 per day for 14–20 days, NZ$ 98 for 21 days plus. Ford *Telstar* (or similar 5-seater automatic) NZ$ 159 per day for 1–2 days, NZ$ 118 per day for 4–13 days, NZ$ 115 for 14–20 days, NZ$ 113 for 21 days plus. All prices include unlimited mileage.

Cigarettes. NZ$ 5.50 for a packet of 20.

Farm holidays. NZ$ 72 per day.

Hairdressers. *Man's* haircut NZ$ 10–20. *Woman's* shampoo and set or blow-dry NZ$ 25–45, permanent wave NZ$ 35–120.

Hotels. Budget-class NZ$ 55–75, medium NZ$ 90–120, superior NZ$ 150 upwards (twin occupancy per night).

Motel flats. NZ$ 50–90 (twin occupancy).

Motor inns. NZ$ 90–150 (twin occupancy).

Taxis. Meter starts at NZ$ 2, plus NZ$ 1.39 per km.

Trains. Wellington-Auckland NZ$ 123, Christchurch–Dunedin NZ$ 55, Christchurch–Invercargill NZ$ 88.

Youth hostels. NZ$ 8–19 per night.

An A–Z Summary
of Practical Information and Facts

ACCOMMODATION. See also under CAMPING, You'll find hotels of international standard in all the top tourist areas.

Motor inns are ideal if you're on a driving holiday. They offer single rooms/family suites. Most have restaurants with licenses to serve alcohol.

Motel flats, self-catering accommodation, are usually equipped with a fridge, cooker, pots and pans, crockery, cutlery and a few essentials like instant coffee, tea, milk and sugar. Some motels have a small store in the grounds, many have a swimming/thermal pool. Motel flats are mainly self-service (i.e., the beds are made for you but you do your own washing up). In units where cooking facilities are not provided, breakfast is included.

Farm holidays give you a glimpse of the real New Zealand. The choice is huge, from dairy farms to high country sheep runs and even deer farms. You can stay on the coast or near major scenic attractions. Your hosts provide three meals a day and treat you in every way as a welcome guest. You can help out on the farm, ride, fish, swim or play tennis. Self-catering farm holidays are also available.

For details, ask for the *Accommodation Guide*, available from New Zealand Tourist and Publicity Offices in the country and overseas.

Youth Hostels. Open to members of the Youth Hostels Association. Non-members may stay at the manager's discretion and are charged more than members. The maximum stay at each is three nights, but can be more if the hostel is not fully booked. Reservations are advisable during school-holiday periods. Write to the warden of your chosen hostel in advance, enclosing the fee and a stamped, addressed envelope, or make a telephone booking in advance. For details and a list of addresses, contact the Youth Hostels Association of New Zealand, 28 Worcester Street, PO Box 436, Christchurch or Australis House, 36 Customs Street East, Auckland.

The *Youth Hostels Guide* contains a list of addresses, phone numbers and prices, as well as a map pinpointing the location of each hostel.

Privately owned 'backpackers' hostels', offering budget accommo-dation in competition with the YHA hostels, are found in most cities and tourist-region towns. Free guides are available at information centres. **111**

A **AIRPORTS.** International flights serve Wellington, Auckland and Christchurch.

Wellington (WLG) International (Rongotai), 8km south-east of the city centre. Transport to city by taxi or bus (15 minutes, every 30 minutes from 8am to 5pm Monday to Friday).

Auckland (AKL) International (Mangere), 22km south of the city centre. Transport to city by taxi or bus (45 minutes, every 30 minutes from 6.45am to 8.45pm daily.)

Christchurch (CHC) International, 10km north-west of the city centre. Transport to city by taxi or bus (25 minutes, every hour from 6am to 8pm daily, with half-hourly services at peak times on weekdays).

All three airports have baggage trolleys, hotel reservation desks, car-hire offices, banks, information centres and souvenir and duty-free shops.

When your aircraft lands, you'll be asked to remain seated while the cabin is sprayed by health officials (the spray used has been approved by the World Health Organization). This measure helps to keep New Zealand free of many plant and animal diseases which could seriously affect agriculture. For the same reason, your baggage will be thoroughly checked. Do not attempt to take in seeds or foodstuffs (there's an 'amnesty box' for discarding any oversights). Footwear worn on overseas farms, used camping equipment and souvenirs from certain parts of the world (cane baskets, animal skins, etc.) which may contain insect eggs are subject to controls. Feathers used in angling flies are also suspect. If necessary, contaminated articles will be treated on the spot or held up to 48 hours for fumigation. These measures are courteously but strictly enforced.

Passengers leaving New Zealand must pay an airport development tax.

B **BABY-SITTERS.** The reception desk at your hotel or motel will arrange for a reliable baby-sitter. Campers will find plenty of sympathetic parents to help out.

C **CAMPING.** Since much of New Zealand's appeal lies out of doors, camping is the ideal way to see the country. Many people hire a caravan (trailer) or camper van. Luxury vehicles come equipped with heating and toilet facilities, a fridge, cooker and kitchen utensils.

Motor camps near main resorts are well maintained and fitted with electricity and toilet and laundry facilities. Campers provide their own tents and equipment, available for hire from firms throughout the country. Some camps offer cabins ranging from the purely basic to the equivalent of a modest apartment. For these you provide your own blankets, linen and cutlery. Prices vary according to standard and season. Advance reservations are necessary during the peak season (December to April).

Camping sites have fewer facilities than motor camps and are located in remoter areas. Ask for the Automobile Association's *Motor Camp and Cabin Booklet* and the official directory issued by the Camp and Cabin Association of New Zealand. The AA also provides a list of caravan rental companies. If you want to camp on farmland, ask the farmer's permission. Should you set up camp away from organized sites, pay scrupulous attention to fire precautions (see under FIRE HAZARDS), close farm gates behind you and remove all rubbish when you leave. It's a good idea to invest in a 'thermette', a small gadget for boiling water rapidly in the open. In your preparations, make allowances for New Zealand's unpredictable weather.

CAR HIRE and DRIVING. Reliable international and local firms offer a range of vehicles for hire. You'll need an approved national or international driving licence. The minimum age is 21, though some firms will waive the age restriction at the manager's discretion.

Chauffeur-driven vehicles are available for short or long trips. Taxi companies also provide the services of experienced driver-guides. Rates include basic mileage plus the driver's living expenses and vary according to the number of passengers. If you rent a mobile home or camper van between May and December, you may benefit from a considerable off-season discount.

The New Zealand Automobile Association offers free services and privileges to members of accredited overseas motoring organizations. It also handles vehicle insurance. Through the Association you can make reservations for accommodation and the inter-island ferry.

Main offices are located at:

Wellington: 342–352 Lambton Quay (PO Box 1053); tel. 473 8738
Auckland: 99 Albert Street (PO Box 5); tel. 377 4660
Christchurch: 210 Hereford Street (PO Box 994); tel. 379 1280

C **Driving regulations.** Traffic keeps to the left. Seat belts are compulsory for all passengers eight years of age and over. Helmets are compulsory for motorcyclists and pillion passengers. Maximum speed limits are 50kph in built-up areas unless otherwise indicated, 100kph on motorways and on roads outside built-up areas. Road hazards include possums, quail and large flocks of sheep and cows, so go carefully. If you encounter the latter, take your time and edge through them, or get someone to walk ahead to clear a path for the vehicle. Where there are no pavements (sidewalks), walk facing the oncoming traffic.

Distances. Here are some approximate road distances in kilometres:

North Island, from Wellington to:

Auckland 660	Napier 335
Hamilton 535	Rotorua 460

South Island, from Christchurch to:

Dunedin 360	Mt Cook 330
Invercargill 580	Queenstown 485

To convert kilometres to miles:

Distance

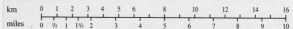

CHILDREN. Apart from particularly strenuous river-rafting trips and hikes, beyond the capacities of under-twelves, children can participate in most adult activities. They'll find plenty of their own age anxious to have them join in spontaneous games of cricket, rounders, softball or football. Even the smallest community has a children's playground. Hotels and motels can provide games for wet-weather amusement. Public bars are prohibited to young people under the age of 20.

To many overseas children, New Zealand seems like a wonderful adventure, with trees to be climbed, creeks to be explored, and animals to be fed and petted – all in a very child-oriented society. But take care that they don't wander off into the bush or swim unattended, even unsupervised paddling can be dangerous on some unprotected ocean beaches. Make sure your children always wear life-jackets when boating, and that they stay on the paths in thermal areas. Some appealing-looking native berries are poisonous. Should a child get lost, you can be sure someone will take care of him or her. But if a child vanishes in a beach, bush or river area, telephone the police immediately from the nearest house and enlist the help of anyone in the vicinity.

CIGARETTES, CIGARS, TOBACCO. Major international brands are for sale at tobacconists, in dairies, at some grocery stores and from slot machines. New Zealand is a non-smokers' paradise. Smoking is illegal in all public buildings and workplaces (other than in a few prescribed areas) and on all public transport.

CLOTHING. In summer (November–February) conventional lightweight clothing is comfortable, and shorts and tee-shirts are common. Some hotels and hotel bars frown on jeans, thong sandals and bare feet, and request men to wear ties.

In mountain and bush areas, be prepared for changes in the weather and take appropriate footwear. New Zealanders love to go barefoot, but they're used to it. You and your children may find it harder walking on sharp shells, prickly lawns and hot pavements, so you would do best to wear open sandals.

A raincoat and umbrella are bound to come in useful.

COMMUNICATIONS

Post office. Main post offices (or NZ Post shops, as they are known) offer stationery retailing as well as postal, telegram and fax services. In rural areas the general store doubles as post office. Opening hours: 9am to 5pm, Monday to Friday.

Telephone. Local calls made from private phones are free. Card-operated public (pay) phones with trunk (toll) and international direct dialling are located throughout the country. Cards in various denominations are readily available, usually at nearby shops. A few coin-operated public phones remain at airports and rail stations.

All New Zealand phone numbers have been converted to seven digits, so if you think a telephone number may have changed, dial the Help Desk (tel. 0155), free of charge, to check what the number is now.

C **COMPLAINTS.** Your first recourse should be the proprietor of the establishment in question, or your hotel manager, travel agency representative or tour operator, as appropriate.

While there is no public tourism watchdog, there is a Minister of Tourism and a Minister of Consumer Affairs. In the unusual event of your being unable to obtain satisfaction, their offices should be interested in hearing from you.

CONVERSION CHARTS

New Zealand uses the metric system. For distance measures, see under CAR HIRE AND DRIVING.

Temperature

Length

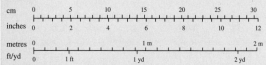

Weight

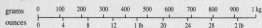

Fluid measures

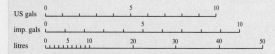

CRIME and THEFT. If you take reasonable precautions, there is no reason to expect anything untoward to occur. Lock your car and don't leave tempting articles visible inside. Keep valuables in the hotel safe and don't abandon possessions on the beach while you swim. Any theft should be reported immediately to hotel authorities, who will contact the police. Drug offences are treated very seriously.

CUSTOMS FORMALITIES. Citizens of Western European countries

and the US and Canada are entitled to a three-month visa-free entry into New Zealand, extendable to up to one year on presentation of passport, plus evidence of sufficient funds for their stay, onward bookings and the visa needed for the next country on the itinerary. However, those who know in advance that their stay will exceed three months are well advised to obtain a visa, at minimal cost, from the embassy or consulate in the country of departure. No vaccination certificates are required.

Here are the main items you may take into New Zealand duty-free and, upon your return home, into your own country:

Into:	Cigarettes		Cigars		Tobacco	Spirits		Wine
New Zealand	200	or	50	or	250g*	1.1 l	and	4.5 l
Australia	200	or	250g	or	250g	1 l	or	1 l
Canada	200	and	50	and	900g	1.1 l	or	1.1 l
Eire	200	or	50	or	250g	1 l	and	2 l
UK	200	or	50	or	250g	1 l	and	2 l
USA	200	and	100	and	**	1 l	or	1 l

* Or a combination of these three products up to 250 grams or ½lb.
** A reasonable quantity.

Concealable firearms (revolvers, automatic pistols, etc.) are not admitted. For any other type of firearms and for ammunition you'll need a licence, issued by police officers on arrival. The import of narcotics is prohibited. See also under AIRPORTS.

Currency restrictions. There is no restriction on the import or export of foreign or local currency.

ELECTRIC CURRENT. 230 volts, 50 hertz, AC. The majority of hotels have sockets for 110-volt AC electric razors. Three-pin flat plugs are in use throughout the country.

EMBASSIES. Diplomatic and consular representatives in Wellington:
Australian High Commission: 72–78 Hobson Street, Thorndon (Private Bag); tel. 473 6411

E **British High Commission:** Hill Street, Thorndon (PO Box 1812); tel. 472 6049

Canadian High Commission: ICI House, Molesworth Street (PO Box 12049); tel. 473 9577

Japanese Embassy: 7th floor, Norwich Insurance House, 3–11 Hunter Street (PO Box 6340); tel. 473 1540

US Embassy: 29 Fitzherbert Terrace (Private Bag); tel. 472 2068

EMERGENCIES. Dial 111 and ask for police, fire or ambulance. Emergency numbers for doctors, dentists, hospitals and local authorities are given in the front of local telephone directories and posted in telephone boxes. Police control call-outs for search and rescue services in the bush.

F **FIRE HAZARDS.** Fire poses a constant threat to New Zealand's natural beauty. In summer, scrub and grass are tinder-dry and the slightest spark can start a blaze. Don't throw matches or cigarettes from car windows, and don't light fires in restricted areas. Beach barbecues are tolerated so long as you're a safe distance from trees – but be sure to shelter the fire well from sea breezes, a chance cinder can set a whole bush-bound coast alight. Always extinguish a fire carefully by dowsing it with water or covering it with earth. Glass can concentrate the sun's rays and start fires; store empty bottles in the shade and take them with you when you leave.

FLIGHTSEEING. 'Flightseeing' in light aircraft is one of the pleasures of a New Zealand holiday. It is especially recommended for the outstanding scenic areas of Rotorua, Mt Cook, Fox and Franz Josef glaciers, Queenstown and Milford Sound. Alpine flights use special planes with retractable skis for landing on snow and ice.

H **HEALTH and MEDICAL CARE.** Both public and private health services are of a high standard. Hotels and motels usually have a doctor on call. Doctors are listed separately at the front of telephone directories.

In the case of accident all visitors are entitled to compensation, which covers reasonable expenses such as doctor's fees and hospitalization. As this doesn't apply to illness, you should take out a travel insurance in your country of residence. New Zealand has health agreements with several countries (including Britain), so check the situation before leaving home.

If you've flown a long distance, take it easy for a day or two to get over the jet lag, which is often more pronounced on the second day.

Guard against sunburn. Use a sun-screen lotion if you're out of doors for any length of time in the summer.

Sandflies can be a menace, so keep them away with insect repellent. Wasps have become a major problem in some bush areas. Trampers should carry anti-histamine medication as a precaution.

Pharmacies (chemists) are open 9am to 5.30pm, Monday to Thursday, until 9pm on Friday, and Saturday morning. After hours, the address of an emergency chemist is posted on the door of all other pharmacies.

HITCH-HIKING. It's perfectly acceptable to hitch a ride – but, as in most parts of the world, women should not hitch-hike alone, nor at night or in isolated places. It's illegal to hitch-hike on New Zealand motorways.

LANGUAGE. Both English and Maori, the language of the indigenous people, are official languages, but English is the most commonly spoken. Many of the place names are in Maori. Pronunciation is not difficult once you master the vowels, which often occur alongside each other but are pronounced separately:

a as in c**a**	**o** like **aw** in p**aw**	**i** like **ee** in b**ee**n
e as in m**e**n	**u** like **oo** in m**oo**n	

The only complex sounds are **wh**, pronounced more or less like **f**, and **ng**, pronounced like the **ing** in si**ng**ing. Syllables are given equal stress.

The following are some of the more common Maori words and phrases that you're likely to hear:

ao	cloud	**patu**	club
atua	god	**rangatira**	chief
haere-mai	welcome	**raupo**	bulrush
haere-ra	goodbye	**tangata**	human being
hau	wind	**tangi**	mourning
ika	fish		(funeral)
kai	food	**tapu**	sacred
ka pai	good	**tohunga**	priest
kia ora	good luck	**umu**	earth oven

119

L	mana	prestige	**utu**	satisfaction;
	maunga	mountain		revenge
	moko	tattoo	**wai**	water
	motu	island	**waka**	canoe
	pa	fortified	**waiata**	song
		village	**whare**	house

If you feel by now that you have gained a certain proficiency, try yourself on one of the longest place-names in the world, attached to a hill in the Hawke's Bay area. In its *shortened* version it's called Taumatawhaka-tangihangakoauauotamateapokaiwhenuakitanatahu. It means 'where Tamatea of the big knees, the man who slid down, climbed and consumed mountains and is known as the landeater, played the flute to his beloved'.

LAUNDRY and DRY-CLEANING. Most motels and some hotels have do-it-yourself laundry facilities. Large hotels provide laundry and dry-cleaning services. At local laundries and dry-cleaners your clothing will usually be returned in 48 hours. You pay a little extra for a same-day or one-hour dry-cleaning rush service.

M **MAPS.** Tourist offices and car-hire companies distribute free maps. The New Zealand Automobile Association also produces regional maps; a nominal sum is charged for North and South Island maps.

MEETING PEOPLE. Even if you're on your own, you will never be lonely. New Zealanders are warm-hearted and hospitable. You'll strike up conversations in all sorts of places, and may well make friends for life.

MONEY MATTERS
Currency. The New Zealand dollar (NZ$) is divided into 100 cents.
  Coins: 5, 10, 20, 50 cents; 1, 2 dollars.
  Banknotes: 5, 10, 20, 50 and 100 dollars.
For currency restrictions, see CUSTOMS AND ENTRY REGULATIONS.

Banking hours. 9am to 4.30pm, Monday to Friday.

Credit cards and traveller's cheques. Internationally recognized credit cards are widely accepted, and traveller's cheques can be cashed in banks,
the bigger hotels and tourist-oriented shops.

NEWSPAPERS and MAGAZINES. The country publishes no nation-wide paper, but all the main centres have morning dailies. The *New Zealand Herald* (Auckland) and the *Dominion* (Wellington) are widely available outside their own areas. Local dailies, usually evening editions, are published in smaller places. They can all be bought from newsagents, from street-vendors or from 'honesty box' stands where you drop in the appropriate coins and serve yourself.

New Zealand's major resort areas produce papers of regional interest for visitors, which include historical background and information about sightseeing, restaurants and current events. You can obtain them free at hotels and tourist offices.

PHOTOGRAPHY. All brands of film (including Super 8) are available at photographic stores and chemist shops (pharmacies). Processing is rapid and reliable. Video cassettes are also readily available.

PUBLIC HOLIDAYS. When Christmas, Boxing Day or New Year's Day falls on a Saturday or Sunday, the statutory public holiday is observed on the following Monday. National holidays are:

New Year's Day	January 1
New Year Holiday	January 2
Waitangi Day	February 6
Good Friday	movable
Easter Monday	movable
ANZAC Day	April 25
Queen's Birthday	first Monday in June
Labour Day	fourth Monday in October
Christmas Day	December 25
Boxing Day	December 26

RADIO and TELEVISION. There are two national non-commercial radio networks, and many regional or local commercial stations on the AM (medium wave) and FM wave bands. There are also three national television channels. A UHF network of three subscription channels (sport, news, films) is available in most areas, and main centres have regional channels. Most hotel and motel rooms have radio and television. Some hotels subscribe to satellite TV programmes from overseas stations.

R **RELIGIOUS SERVICES.** New Zealand has no state church, but most religions are represented in its population. The daily papers give details of addresses and times of services.

S **SHOPPING HOURS.** Shops are usually open from 9am to 5.30pm, Monday to Thursday, till 9pm on Friday, and till 12.30pm on Saturday (4.30pm in larger centres). Small suburban dairies, most large shopping centres, and many shops in tourist resorts are also open on Sundays.

SPORTS CALENDAR

	Summer [N D J F]	Autumn [M A M J]	Winter [J A]	Spring [S O]
Trout Fishing				
Lake Rotorua	(————Open season all through the year————)			
Lake Taupo	(————Open season all through the year————)			
Lakes Tarawera and Okataina	(–Open season October to June–) Early Best	(Best Fish)	(Closed season)	Open
Southern Lakes	(–Open October to May–)		(–Closed season–)	Open
Rest of New Zealand	(–Open season–)		(–Closed season–)	Open
Big Game Fishing	(——Open season——)			
Winter Sports			(–South Island–) (North Island)	
Mountain Climbing South Island Mountains		(-Climbing-) Season	(——Snow covered——)	
Game				
Wild Duck and Swan		3 weeks		
Pheasant and Quail		2 months		
Wallaby, Goat and Pig	(————Open season all through the year————)			

TAXIS. There's a 24-hour service operating from taxi ranks or on call by telephone. Cars are metered.

TIME DIFFERENCES. New Zealand is 12 hours ahead of Greenwich
Mean Time. Clocks advance one hour from the last Sunday in October to
the first Sunday in March. The chart below shows the time differences
between New Zealand and various cities.

	Los Angeles	New York	London	Sydney	Wellington
Jan	3pm *(Fri)*	6pm *(Fri)*	11pm *(Fri)*	10am *(Sat)*	noon *(Sat)*
July	5pm *(Fri)*	8pm *(Fri)*	1am *(Sat)*	10am *(Sat)*	noon *(Sat)*

TIPPING and SERVICE CHARGES. A 12½% Goods and Service Tax
(GST) is levied on all goods and services It is usually included in the quot-
ed price – but not always. Tipping is not encouraged, but with growing
numbers of overseas visitors it is no longer unusual and is appreciated if
offered in a personal way. Taxi drivers do not expect tips.

TOILETS. Generally labelled 'Gentlemen' and 'Ladies' or identified by
male or female symbols, toilets are found in hotel lobbies, shopping centres, large stores, restaurants, museums and cinemas. Built-up areas have
clearly marked public 'restrooms'; they are also located in picnic spots
along main roads and at the most frequented beaches.

TOURIST INFORMATION OFFICES. The New Zealand Tourism
Department maintains marketing and information offices overseas (the
domestic offices do not cater for consumers). There are overseas offices in:

Australia: 84 Pitt Street, Sydney, NSW 2000; tel. (02) 231-57137

Canada: New Zealand Consulate, Suite 1260, 701 West Georgia Street,
Vancouver, BC; tel. (604) 684-2117

Japan: 2F, Toho Twin Tower Building, 1-5-2- Yurakucho,
Chiyoda-Ku, Tokyo 100; tel. (03) 508-9981

UK: New Zealand House, Haymarket, London SW1Y 4TQ;
tel. (0171) 930 8422

USA: 501 Santa Monica Blvd, Santa Monica, CA 90401;
tel. (213) 395-5813

T **Singapore:** 13 Nassim Road, Singapore 1025; tel. 235 9966

Hong Kong: 3414 Jarden House, Connaught Place, Central Hong Kong; tel. 5260141

New Zealand embassies abroad also supply travel information.

Within the country: Visitor Information Centres have been established in most towns throughout New Zealand.

TRANSPORT

Buses. Local buses run according to a published timetable. Fares are calculated according to the number of 'sections' travelled. Some city shuttle buses have 'honesty boxes' into which you drop the required amount. (Wellington has electric trains to northern suburbs.)

Modern coaches provide countryside service. They are not normally air-conditioned, but are heated in winter. Budget-priced 'backpacker' coaches also cover major routes.

Trains. Mainline rail services are comfortable, and express trains serve on the main overnight and long-distance daytime routes. The *Northerner* travels overnight between Auckland and Wellington Sunday to Friday, while the *Overlander* makes the same run in daylight every day. The *Kamai Express* operates between Auckland and Tauranga, and the *Geyserland* between Auckland and Rotorua. Refreshments are included on both services, and a commentary on passing sights is provided. The *Southerner* connects Christchurch and Invercargill Monday to Friday. Refreshments are available. The *Coastal Pacific* runs between Picton and Christchurch, and the *Tranz-Alpine Express* between Greymouth and Christchurch. Both are renowned scenic journeys. Both run daily; refreshments are available.

Inquire about the New Zealand Railways Travelpass. You can buy one valid for either 8, 15 or 22 days. The pass entitles holders to unlimited travel on the national rail network, as well as on coach and ferry lines operated by New Zealand Railways. It's also good for discounts on private rail lines and at certain chain hotels.

If you are a member of the Youth Hostels Association (see under ACCOMMODATION), ask the Association for information about the special **124** rail discounts available to you.

Ferries. Inter-island car ferries between Wellington and Picton link the North and South islands. The crossing takes 3 hours; there are cafeteria and bar facilities. There is also a regular passenger ferry from Bluff, the port of Invercargill, to Oban on Stewart Island. It is advisable to book in advance for all ferries, especially during holiday periods. Some sailings are cancelled during the low season.

WALKING TRACKS. Write to DOC, PO Box 10–420, Wellington, for information on tramping tracks and shorter walks. Fees are charged at most DOC huts and campsites. The most popular tramping tracks are:

Abel Tasman Coastal Track (30km): An easy 3–4 day walk along sandy coastal areas and through subtropical forest. A boat can drop off or pick up visitors at any beach along the coast. For details of guided walks, contact Abel Tasman National Park Enterprises.

Routeburn Track (39km): The 3-day track begins in beech forest and rises to 1,277m, with alpine vegetation and amazing views. The best time for this walk is summer (October–May), so you avoid snow. For guided walks, contact Routeburn Walks Ltd.

Milford Track (52km): Access by boat; open late October to the middle of April. The walk is mainly along gently sloping valleys, except for a steep climb to the McKinnon pass. This is the only track that must be booked by independent walkers – contact DOC, Te Anau. For guided walk, contact South Pacific Hotel Corporation.

For less-travelled but equally beautiful walks try:

Whirinaki Track: 2–4 days' easy walking, suitable for families.

Lake Waikaremoana Track (43km): 4–5 days' easy walk round the lake, through forest. Worthwhile excursion to Korokoro Falls.

St James Walkway (66km): A fairly easy 5-day track through forest and sheep-farm land, ending near hot springs.

WATER. Tap water is safe. Bottled mineral water is also available. The internal microscopic parasite Giardia, which is present in some rivers and lakes, can cause serious stomach illness. If you are collecting water directly from rivers or lakes, the best way to avoid contracting this disease is to boil, filter or chemically treat your drinking water.

Index

An asterisk (*) next to a page number indicates a map reference. Where there is more than one set of page references, the one in bold type refers to the main entry.

INDEX